God's Questions
and Answers

Also by Robert W. Bailey:

THE MINISTER AND GRIEF

God's Questions and Answers

CONTEMPORARY STUDIES IN
Malachi

Robert W. Bailey

A Crossroad Book
THE SEABURY PRESS/NEW YORK

1977
The Seabury Press
815 Second Avenue
New York, N.Y. 10017

Printed in the United States of America

Library of Congress Cataloging in Publication Data
Bailey, Robert W
God's Question and Answers
"A Crossroad Book."
Includes bibliographical references.
1. Bible. O.T. Malachi—Meditations. I. Title.
BS1675.4.B34   224'.99'06   76-56513
ISBN 0-8164-1231-6 78-96 42

To my wife, Mary Frances,
through whose love, encouragement,
and radiant Christian life my life finds meaning

Contents

Malachi

Grim messengers of God,
Nameless down aeons of forgotten years,
He thought it enough to write his name
In the Father's Book of Remembrance.

Others saw the shadow;
He groped for the light,
And found it.
"God has forgotten," they said,
"The people of His love."
He answered: "God remembers;
"He will return
"To those who return to Him."
Cynics mocked him:
"God knows and yet we suffer?
"Your God is a weakling
"Or, possibly, afraid."
(His God a weakling?)
"No," he thundered.

God's flaming day is near;
"It is darkened in dawning
"By man's unrighteousness.
"I will send my messenger,
"Saith the Lord of Hosts;
"And who may abide his coming?
"Who shall stand when he appears?
"For he is like a forger's fire
"Or a fuller's acid."

He saw the sins of his friends
And denounced them fearlessly:
"Every man dealt treacherously with his brother,"
And priests, in the name of **God**,
Called mummery religion.
He saw its hollowness.
"The heathen," he sighed
"Serve God more truly
"Than the children of His choice."

Foredreaming the faith of the future,
He knew and preached the truth:
One honors his Father
When he loves and serves his brother:
"Have not all of us one Father?"

His was the shining vision,
The task of the pioneer:
He blazed the trail of a Brother
Who fared beyond the sun
And fathomed its mystery:
"I am the light of the world.
"God is a spirit,
"And they that worship Him
"Must worship Him in spirit
"And in truth."[1]

                                Earl Marlatt

Preface

People of all ages and walks of life are out of touch with God today. They tend to do their own thing and go their own way. It is not that modern men are irreligious. they have many religions, worshipping many different things and people, but they are living apart from God. They have unanswered questions of God, and yet they have not heard God's questions of them.

The prophet Malachi lived just over four centuries before Christ in an environment not unlike that of many places in the United States today. His was an age when God was not looked upon with favor, and spokesmen of God were not given much attention. Malachi realized a prophet could no longer get a hearing simply by declaring: "Thus saith the Lord. . . ." As a result he adopted a new technique for proclaiming God's message.

The rhetorical question-answer formula was the method Malachi employed in his proclamation. His style was so impressive that some scholars have called him the Hebrew Socrates. Malachi raised God's questions for the religious people, and then he proceeded to give God's answers to the questions. The format he most frequently used was to make a charge or declaration followed by a question and reply. He then concluded with an application of a specific truth on that issue. The question-answer passages in Malachi's writing constitute eight bases of life that are misinterpreted.[1] He has given religious people eight checkpoints to determine whether or not they are living in a proper, acceptable relationship with God.

This book stems from Malachi's writing, but it is not designed to be a commentary. Rather, it is an attempt to reconstruct the context of the divine-human relationship, which had become distorted in the days of the prophet, in order that modern man might see how he has falsified his own relationship with God. There are many similarities between Malachi's day and ours—particularly the inflationary economy and the indifferent religion—even though some twenty-five centuries have intervened. One chapter is devoted to each of Malachi's question-answer sets, with the exception of the lengthy third one, which is described in chapters 3 and 4.

The prophet Malachi gave some insights into how lifeless religion could be revitalized. The same need for authentic religious regeneration exists today for Christians individually and collectively. Though an ancient document, Malachi's writing has tremendous impact for a decadent, complacent, and apathetic religious nation in the closing years of the twentieth century. If modern man can internalize the positive concepts of Malachi, he can establish a vital, meaningful relationship with God.

The text quoted before each chapter is taken from the Revised Standard Version, copyright © 1946, 1952, 1971, 1973. My own translation is often used in the body of the book. The initials RSV will be used to distinguish clearly the quotations from that translation.

Questions for thought and discussion and suggestions for action—for individuals and/or groups—appear at the end of each chapter. Through the stimulus of Malachi it is intended that God's questions and answers might be encountered by modern man.

God's Questions
and Answers

The oracle of the word of the Lord to Israel by Malachi, *"I have loved you," says the Lord. But you say, "How hast thou loved us?"* "Is not Esau Jacob's brother?" says the Lord. "Yet I have loved Jacob but I have hated Esau; I have laid waste his hill country and left his heritage to jackals of the desert." If Edom says, "We are shattered but we will rebuild the ruins," the Lord of hosts says, "They may build, but I will tear down, till they are called the wicked country, the people with whom the Lord is angry for ever." Your own eyes shall see this, and you shall say, "Great is the Lord beyond the border of Israel!" (Mal. 1:1–5) RSV

1

Being Sure About Love

The young college coed, living away from home for the first time in her life, was impressed by the attention shown her by a flashy upperclassman. He reassuringly told her after several dates: "Anything is okay if you love someone." When she tried to draw some limits to expression of love, he declared, somewhat angrily: "Well, if you love me, you are going to have to show it! You must prove to me you love me by doing what I say!"

How many young lives have been wrecked by a manipulative operator like that student? The even more basic questions are: What is meant by the use of the term *love*? How is love to be defined? The use of the word *love* is often naive and superficial. "Love" is called on to express almost everything:

excitement over an animal—"I love that cute kitten"
appreciation of new clothes—"I love this dress"
admiration of a color—"I love blue"
effort at manipulation—"I'll love you if . . ."
expression of emotion—"I'd love to hit you"
acknowledgment of parent-child relationship—"I love you, Daddy"
description of God-man relationship—"God loves us, we love God"

How overworked and misused is the word *love!* The very diversity of its usage has cheapened its meaning and dulled its focus.

The Hebrews and Greeks were not so poverty-stricken in terms of descriptive words. Each language had more than one word for love, and each reserved a word rich in meaning to express the feeling God had for his people. The Hebrews' unending loving-kindness, *ahav*, and the Greeks' godlike love, *agape*, describe in unmistakable terms the love that God offers man. This love of God is unselfishly, freely given to man, who does not deserve it and only receives it as a gift. Across the centuries man has had a difficult time perceiving the nature of God's love and making a genuine response to it. The truth that God's love has no strings attached has never really soaked into man's mind. It seems as though modern man is not sure about God's love.

The prophet Malachi demonstrated real insight into the feelings of man of every generation, especially modern man. Through his question-answer methodology he indicted the false attitude toward God, the false reasoning used to view God. It is significant that the last book of the Old Testament opens with a statement as profound as:

"I have loved you," says the Lord. (Mal. 1:2)

The word for love is one which indicates a close, personal relationship. This statement points to the heart of the covenant established between God and the people of Israel under Moses. The simple declaration of God's unending love is the basis of all other appeals on the part of Yahweh God. His love for Israel should be both the model and the motive for Israel's response to him.

Malachi came back with the people's response to God's statement of love. They ask:

"How have you [God] loved us?" (Mal. 1:2)

With an attitude that is basically false, certainly false reasoning will be used, and likely, dishonest conclusions reached. Undoubtedly the people were upset in the midst of their troubles. They complained about what God had not done. They blamed all their troubles on him. In spite of the quality of his love for the Jewish people emphasized by the graphic Hebrew word, *ahav*, used to describe it, the prophet reported that the Jews questioned if God really did love them.

A closer look at what was taking place in Malachi's day reveals startling similarities to our time. The people were living at the close of a century of religious indifference. This era had begun soon after the first Jews returned from the Babylonian Exile in 537 B.C. While in Babylon they had learned to do without the Temple. Upon their return to Jerusalem, they spent some twenty years in half-hearted labor to restore the Temple. And it was far from being as glorious as Solomon's had been! They had worked with the hopes of greatness when they completed their labor. They had been opposed during this time by the Samaritans.

Now a century after the initial return from Babylon the earlier prophecies about the glorious, restored nation were not fulfilled. Malachi's contemporaries were still ruled by foreigners. They had to pay taxes to Persia and give its army provisions. They had limited resources, for they had experienced crop failure, drought, pestilence, and poverty. On top of all this, although they had been taught that piety was rewarded with prosperity and impiety with adversity, several decades before Malachi there arose a group of godless men who became unscrupulously wealthy. During this century the world balance of power was moving not to Judea, but from Asia to powerful Greece.

Left to themselves and the petty hostilities of their neighbors, the Jews sank into disillusionment, disappointment, decay, and disinterest. In the small part of Jerusalem that had been rebuilt, the internal conditions went from bad to worse. Interestingly enough, they had entered this era with a sense of distinction.

> In exile they had suffered God's anger, and been purged by it. But out of discipline often springs pride—no subtler temptation of the human heart! The returned Israel felt this to the quick, and it unfitted them for encountering the disappointment and hardship which followed on the completion of the Temple. . . . Their pride was on edge, and they fell, not as at other times of disappointment into despair, but into carelessness and contempt of their duty to God. . . . It led them to despise both His love and His holiness.[1]

The people felt that God did not care about them, so they questioned why they should bother about God. They were filled with bitterness. They felt they had been forgotten by the world and abandoned by God. First religious fervor declined and then morals decayed. The people were practicing sorcery, adultery, false swearing, and much more. Clearly they disregarded God's love and failed to offer him their love and their lives in service to him. They acted as though they thought all that was required of them was to restore the Temple, erect an important place of worship, reinstitute the sacrificial system of former days—and *then* they would prosper gloriously! They did what they thought was required for greatness, and they were disappointed. When prosperity and strength did not come, they heaped their indifference and animosity upon God. Indeed, they sassed God!

One person has said that Malachi gives a picture of a dying church. The Jews mistakenly thought that their new Temple would assure them success. Modern churchmen have tended to demonstrate their greatest energy in constructing church buildings. Many churches have experienced their greatest growth during times of construction. And now some of those same churches have large, half-filled buildings! From the impressions gained from the history of churches it appears that most people felt that new buildings would assure the church of strength, growth, and success for years to come. But it has not happened that way! The current percentage of the population which attends church, much less belongs to church, is the lowest it has been in several decades. Buildings have never assured authentic worship of God, love of God, or response to God.

Is God to blame for the problems in the churches with declining organizations and vacant buildings? Does he not love the modern churches that are not strong numerically? Once a pulpit committee interviewed me, and someone suggested they were seeking a preacher who would fill their sanctuary on Sunday with a large congregation. I reminded them that God does not call a minister to fill a sanctuary! He did call me, as he has each of his messengers, to be the interpreter and proclaimer of him whom people are to worship. He wants no one worshiping a preacher. He wants people coming with joy before him. Often we have overlooked or misunderstood the full dimensions of the God we claim to worship and serve.

The entire portrait of the Jewish nation has not been completed. They had some legitimate problems, but also during the time of Malachi the nation was united in strength. Actually, for the first time since Solomon died some five hundred years before (ca. 931 B.C.), the North and South were together again. And they were living

in a walled city
in the "holy land"
in the presence of God
with the promised Book—
they had it made!

No longer in exile in Babylon, the whole Jewish nation was united for the first time in half a millennium. There were opportunities for growth in the midst of unprecedented blessings of God. And instead of emphasizing what God had done, the bitter people asked wherein did God love them. They pointed out that they had no crops, no king, no power, and no prestige. But where do people get the idea that success is spelled with numbers? Love is not *quantity* but *quality*! The prophet said the people were simply not being honest toward God. These were the people who stood within the covenant with God, those who had committed themselves to God. They had accepted the uninterruptable love that is initiated by God. But they dared question if God loved them. How blind they were!

Moss Hart tells the personal story about how a father's love was ignored and rejected. One Christmas Eve for the first time in Moss's life, his father took him to a line of pushcarts full of Christmas toys along a New York City street. As they walked, Moss would pause before a pushcart and comment with constraint, "Look at that chemistry set!" or "There's a stamp album!" or "Look at the printing press!" Each time he said something, his father would ask the man the price, and then without a word they would move on. A couple of times Mr. Hart picked up a toy and looked at it and then at Moss, as if to suggest it as a possibility. But Moss was all of ten years of age, and he had set his heart on a chemistry set, stamp album, or printing press.

These toys were on every pushcart, but the price was always the same. Suddenly Moss looked up and saw that there were only three pushcarts left. His father noticed the same thing. Then Moss heard him jingle some coins in his pocket. In a moment Moss understood everything. His father had somehow gotten about seventy-five cents together to buy him a Christmas present. He had not mentioned it in case there was nothing to be purchased for so small an amount. Moss looked up at his father and saw the despair and disappointment in his eyes, an expression that brought Moss very close to him. He wanted to throw his arms around his father and tell him that the present did not matter, that he understood, that his father's love was better than a chemistry set or a printing press. He wanted to tell his father that he loved him. But instead of such a response, they both stood shivering next to each other. After a brief moment they turned from the last carts and walked silently home. The event of love had been felt, but it was never acknowledged. And so the relationship continued to be limited by barriers of misconception, misunderstanding, and inadequate communication. We, too, are often blind to the love offered us, and we are unwilling to take the risk to return genuine love to others.

Malachi spoke both to the wicked and to the pious. Then, as even today, the seemingly religious, the pious, often quickly questioned whether God loved them and whether he rendered justice. These pseudoreligious people echoed the wicked, who murmured that it seemed vain to serve him. As is always true in interpreting the Bible, it is important to understand the context in which Malachi spoke. He used an extreme exaggeration, as is characteristic of the classic oriental hyperbole, to assert that God does love them (Mal. 1:2-5). The hyperbole was based on the story of the two famous twin brothers Jacob and Esau. In order to stress his point Malachi referred to the people's concept that God loved Jacob (Israel) and hated Esau (Edom). If you read only these verses, you can arrive at an incorrect conclusion that God loves only the Jews and hates the Gentiles. However, what Malachi did was to choose a graphic example his hearers would readily identify with.

In that day the Edomites were about as irreligious, self-sufficient people as could be imagined. They were profane unrepentant, and without ideals or humility. When

Jerusalem fell to Babylon in 586 B.C., the Edomites rejoiced
(Lam. 4:21–22; Ps. 137:7; Obad. 10–14). But the hyperbole
described that in comparison with God's love for Israel, his
favor to Edom seemed like hate. Yet there was not a divine
emotion like human hate, or else God would not have given
Esau a choice blessing (Gen. 27:39–40), and the Edomites
would not have been a powerful nation (Gen. 25:22–26;
Num. 20:14–21). It is important to realize that the Old
Testament doctrine of divine preference of Israel over Edom
developed only after the characters of the nations had
evidenced themselves. The doctrine was a result of historical
experience, viewing the fundamental contrast between Israel
and Edom in basic nature and destiny. It is not right for us to
stamp on Malachi "predestination" of the two nations apart
from their own choice, their own free will.

The Jews misunderstood that God's divine election was for
them to be his servant people. Instead of humility because of
their election, they were arrogantly indifferent to the love of
God. God chose them to be the people who point all others
to him as the One True God. Instead, they rebelled and
spurned the love of God. And then they had the nerve to
question the validity and reality of his love!

In spite of all the evidence to the contrary, God did still
love the Jews, his people. Malachi asserted the futility of
Edom—evil, worldliness, and irreligion incarnated—to be
victorious in opposition to God's will. Evil never merits or
receives favor from God. Malachi concluded his statement
by saying that when the self-righteous Jews are sure that God
does continue to love them, they will confess that he is great
in majesty, power, and grace. Even the non-Jewish people,
the Edomites, the Gentiles will know him as Lord.

The scope of God's love encircles those who have withdrawn from a weakened religious fellowship, those who are
piously irreligious, those who question if God is just, and
those who murmur that it is useless to serve him. God's love

also includes those beyond the institutional church who open their lives to his Lordship. Those who ultimately choose evil instead of God's will, who choose to reject God's love, inevitably accept God's judgment, wrath, and punishment.

Phillips Brooks said that we have become confused about God's love because we have not distinguished between the two forms of his love. One is the natural love he has for all men—the love that calls man into creation, the love that caused him to send Christ into the world. The second form is his approving love. He loves in an approving way those persons he can love, those who respond to him with spiritual loveliness.[2] The blessed ones God invites to come unto him are all of us who accept the abiding love he offers us. The common confusion on word meanings is not limited to love. Many persons have an outmoded view of God—a concept that does not fulfill their needs. Because so many people have never been sure about God's love, they keep trying to find someone to love them, some way to be loved. J. B. Phillips emphasized in his provocative book, *Your God Is Too Small*: "The trouble with many people today is that they have not found a God big enough for modern needs."[3]

Malachi spoke not only to people more than four hundred years prior to Christ. He speaks to every contemporary Christian and every Christian group who are searching for God's love and trying to maintain strength and develop maturity. Malachi reminds modern man that God can work even where there are no numerical evidences of success. In spite of his weakness or poverty every true follower of God in Jesus Christ can perceive that he is still loved by God.

When we are sure about God's love, we know he first loved us. We can then begin to love all men everywhere because God loves them and tells all his people to love them. No longer does modern man have to be dependent upon numbers, nor does he have to fear failure or rejection by God. God will provide the blessings on his terms when man does his work. Today's Christians need not accuse him for their failures or blame him for lack of material, numerical blessings. Instead of questioning if God loves them, instead of trying to get God to prove his love by making them appear bigger and more important, people today need to get their reasoning and attitude in proper perspective. Then they can be sure of God's love and can joyfully declare its full scope. God does love people today, and thus people today can love God and their brothers and sisters.

Questions for Thought and Discussion

1. Reflect on the description of God's love and attempt to formulate a working, personal definition of godlike love.
2. How can you be sure of God's love for you?
3. How can you deepen your love for God?
4. How does a Christian go about revealing his or her love for God to others?
5. What are some attitudes your church should have in order to develop a more loving Christian community?

Suggestions for Action

1. Develop a love fund to minister to the physical needs of church members and community members alike. A special time for giving offerings to this fund might well be at the conclusion of communion, when Christ's commandment to love others as he loves us has been reaffirmed.
2. Train people with loving and ministering skills to work as Christ's undershepherds. They would relate to and minister to the spiritual, physical, and emotional needs of a small

(often geographic or interest-centered) group of Christians.
A minister could be the trainer-coordinator of the undershepherds.

"A son honors his father, and a servant his master. If then I am a father, where is my honor? And if I am a master, where is my fear?" says the Lord of hosts to you, "O priests, who despise my name. You say, 'How have we despised thy name?' " (Mal. 1:6) RSV

2

Contempt for Casual Faith

John Steinbeck wrote a memorable account of people and the
difficulties they experienced in the often-dry nineteenth-
century California country. He concluded his novel *To a
God Unknown* with a close-up of the local priest. After two
days of rain that came just in time to prevent the land from
dying altogether, Father Angelo noted the excitement among
the people. He knew what they were planning to do, for they
had done it before. Anger flared up in him, and he said:
"Only let them start it, and I'll stop them."

He went to the church, got down a heavy crucifix, coated
it with phosphorous so that it could be seen in the dark, and
then waited as night came. It was hard to hear the sounds of
the people in the street over the splashing of the rain. Finally
he began to hear the crescendo of the pounding of the bass
guitar strings and the chanting of many voices joining the
rhythm. He sat and listened. A strong reluctance to intervene
came over him. He could see in his mind how they were
dancing in their bare feet, wearing the skins of animals, and
chanting louder and louder to the point of hysteria. "They'll
be taking off their clothes, and they'll roll in the mud. They'll
be rutting like pigs in the mud," Father Angelo exclaimed. In
the excitement over rain that followed an intense drought,
the people engaged in a wild celebration that turned into a
sexual orgy.

Slowly Father Angelo opened the door and picked up his
crucifix to carry it out among the people. Then he closed the

door, took off his rainwear, and laid down the cross. He muttered: "I couldn't see them in the dark. . . . They'd all get away in the dark." After this rationalization he confessed to himself: "They wanted the rain so, poor children, I'll preach against them on Sunday. I'll give everybody a little penance."[1]

What a sharp, biting word the novelist used to indict a spiritual leader who allowed his casual faith to replace his loyalty to the true God! The priest knew the people were doing wrong. Yet he allowed his anger to subside by falsely reasoning that the people had waited so long for the rain they deserved their time of godless immorality. He justified his inaction by saying he would step on their feet on Sunday and thus make everything right. What a contemptible spiritual leader!

Malachi noted the people first questioned God's love for them, and then they questioned their failure to use God's name properly. Someone may have challenged their religious practices in times past, but never had anyone confronted them so directly as did Malachi. He claimed God said they despised his name. For the Hebrew mind, name and personality were about the same. Malachi was accusing the priests, the religious leaders, of despising God himself! Their shallow faith was contemptible to God. Yet those indifferent, insincere, insensitive leaders pled that they were not guilty and dared ask how they had despised God's name.

As a youngster growing up in the country, I recall hearing my father spin a yarn about the proverbial stubborn mule. It seems one farmer had a mule that always worked well for him. Out of curiosity his neighbor came early one morning to discover how he trained the mule to be so obedient. The man arrived just in time to hear the farmer command the mule to perform. When the mule hesitated, the farmer hit him on the head, right between his eyes, with a two-by-four-inch board. The startled neighbor demanded why in the world he had hit his mule with the big piece of wood. The

farmer replied: "My mule is always willing to work; sometimes I just have to get his attention."

Malachi got the attention of the religious leaders when he
hit them square between the eyes with the accusation that
they despised God. They wanted to back away from any personal responsibility by trying to get a discussion going. They
sought to escape such a dreadful charge. The great German
preacher-theologian Helmut Thielicke noted that such religious discussions are endless, circular affairs, almost always
spawning new discussion. He gave a mental picture to this
ambling religious conversation by saying that "the circle is
ultimately the symbol of non-commitment."[2] Thielicke went
on to say that Jesus' conversations always ended abruptly.
He made a sudden termination of the circular pattern, implying in no uncertain terms that his listener must either leap or
retreat.

Malachi uttered, as Christ would later on, an accusation
around which there was no detour. And contemporary
Christians must clearly indicate to the world that there are
steep walls before which decisions are to be made. Instead of
peddling cheap grace, modern Christians must show the ban-
ner of their Lord and present the message of the Gospels as a
summons away from casual, selfish living. When contempt is
shown for casual faith, all escape avenues are cut off. Instead
of being preoccupied with the shell in which the kernel of
truth is couched, Christians should direct their focus to the
kernel itself.

A familiar proverb was the base of Malachi's assertion:

A son honors his father, and a servant his master.
(Mal. 1:6a) RSV

A son honored his father intensively, gave weight to him,
even if the son was forty or fifty years old! As long as the
father was around, the Hebrew son was expected to honor
his father. A more complete translation of the Hebrew word

for honor indicates that the son should also portray the image of or bear the manifestation of his father. He was to follow his father intensively and take on his identity. Every person would admit a son and a servant owed reverence and obedience, honor and respect to his father and master. But the Hebrews had failed to give what was due to God, the Father and Master of Israel (Jer. 31:9; Isa. 41:8). Born in the image of God, his people were responsible for making their reverence for him apparent internally and externally. God said if he were "Boss," where was his honor and respect? Modern man, like the ancient Hebrews, does not hold God in awe! Some people think God knows only what he is told. Like those people in Malachi's time, modern man is ready and willing to give respect to men, while refusing to give respect to God.

On the surface these words were addressed to the religious leaders, who were considered to be the "soul of the national life."[3] Actually Malachi's charge was pointed to the whole Hebrew nation, which was called a "kingdom of priests" (Exod. 19:6). A priest was one who carried on functions for another, one who pointed people to God. The question of respect for God is sounded to all religious leaders in particular and all who call themselves the children of God in general. No one has respect for religious leaders whose lives do not uphold their profession of faith in God. Likewise, the spiritual level of ordinary people is seldom higher than their religious leaders.

The above paragraph places almost all of us in an awkward position—lay Christians, professional staff members, and elected leaders alike. We all have the responsibility to show God to people, but we have not done it. We all are expected by God to serve him in reverence and awe, but we have not faithfully done it. We have been discovered! Our casual faith has been found in contempt of God! The phrase Malachi used described in Hebrew that the priests were despising God's name not just once, but they were doing it regularly. They had the nerve then to ask:

"How have we despised thy name?" (Mal. 1:6d) RSV

Yet all the time they had been bringing insult and shame to Yahweh God. Malachi drove a nail through the shoes of those who were accustomed to go through the forms of religion without entering into the spirit of communion with God. He indicated they were making all A's on lip service and appearance, but they were scoring zeros on inner commitment. And still they expected to receive God's blessings!

The sins of the spiritual leader are always grave, for the call of God is a high and serious call. People who are seeking God do not find him when the casual faith of religious leaders makes God contemptible. If the **professing** Christian does not enact the reality of his religious words in his life, all he professes means nothing or—even worse—all he says downgrades God.

How does modern man despise God's name? Some people form his name only when they are upset, excited, or happy. How contemptible that hurried "O God" can be! Others allow the name of God to be placed on their lives—calling themselves the children of God—when he does not make one bit of difference to them. God does not want man to advertize or parade his name in a superficial manner. Rather, people who have responded to God should reveal the God who is the center of their lives by the way they live, speak, think, act, play, and plan.

Most people today may reveal their casual faith and be in contempt of God by the immature, false concept of God they possess. Some persons hold the popular view that God is

a resident policeman, often equated with one's conscience,

a leftover parent, against whom one has rebelled, or
a grand old man who is actually too old-fashioned for
    today.

For others God is

meek and mild, offering soft, cheap love and grace,
a God-in-a-box, trapped and packaged for our conveni-
    ence,
a secondhand God, experienced only in books, dramas,
    or friends' accounts, or
a God in the sky, with whom we escape the world, or
    from whom we escape, since he is so far re-
    moved from us.

Some say God is

an unlimited source of power who forces his will,
a selfish being who regrets any advantage man gains,
a withdrawing, indifferent deity who wants nothing to do
    with man, or
an impersonal, abstract idea—the height of achievement or
    perfection.

Can you isolate your personal concept of God? Is your
God like one described above? Have you overlooked that
God is loving, giving, forgiving, and seeking? One person
has summed up our dilemma in saying: "The world is a kind
of spiritual kindergarten where millions of bewildered in-
fants are trying to spell G-O-D with the wrong blocks."[4]
When you call on God's name and when you live in the
world as one of his children, do you actually consider and
understand who God is?

My Hebrew professor, Dr. J. J. Owens of the Southern
Baptist Theological Seminary in Louisville, Kentucky, told
that when he took each of his daughters to enroll in college,

he had her signature added to the bank account he and his wife shared. He told each daughter she could write a check when she needed it. And she was to write the check as if he were there. It should be a check that would make a difference, and she should know her father would approve of it.

Praying—the opportunity of calling on God's name—is a blank check that modern man misuses. People should know God before signing God's name to their request in order that they might do just as God would do. The religious leaders were busy about praying, but Malachi told them they were despising God's name and they were making up their own rules. A thoughtful child of God needs to be in close communication with God and know the principles of his Word by which to live. The Bible is a compass, not a road map. The Bible does not claim to offer exact steps for one to take the rest of his life, nor is the Bible solely about the last five minutes of earth's existence. Rather, like a compass, the Bible points out which direction we should be traveling if we wish to reach God.

Prayer is not a modern computer achievement that man uses to bail himself out of trouble. Prayer must be lived as well as spoken, and our praying must be honest before God. An honest, relevant prayer is specific. As the ancient Job spoke his mind to God, so advocated a seventeenth-century French archbishop who said: "If God bores you, tell Him so."[5] Then we need to be ready to move beyond this level of honesty. We need to be able to realize this boredom is not God's fault but ours. We need to discover from God a sense of meaning and feeling that it matters we are alive. We can sense this feeling as we experience more often those moments that make us unquestionably sure of his companionship with us and his loving-kindness for us.

Many contemporary churches cannot find enough volunteers to carry out a significant education and mission ministry. Yet the members question how they have despised God. Modern Christians say they are too busy to assume leadership in Christian education or to use the opportunities given them to train as leaders. Yet they ask in what ways they are despising God. Christians today, like the religious leaders of Malachi's day, are engaged in false praying—taking the name of God without assuming his character, wanting rights without responsibility, and demanding irresponsible, complete freedom to do and be as they well please. Yet they are bold enough to question how they are expressing casual faith or living in contempt of God. Contemporary Christians are saying by their priorities, their values, their attitudes, and their actions that being a child of God means little or nothing to them—either in terms of happiness and fulfillment, or in terms of purpose and direction. But they still have the nerve to ask how they are despising the name of God! The gist of the story of God and his relationship to man in the Bible is not God's duties to man but the responsibility of the duties of sonship before God.

Maybe in no way is modern man more in contempt of God than when he reacts as did Steinbeck's Father Angelo. How often do you feel the desire

> to be stirred to a religious height,
> to have your guilt level raised,
> to have your toes stepped on, and then
> to be forgiven and released to go and do as you please?

Modern man might not be running around barefoot in the rain engaging in sexual orgies, but he is in contempt of God when he hypocritically recites a prayer for God's mercy and guidance while only fulfilling a perfunctory ritual. Contemporary religious people do not have to be immoral by society's standards in order to be guilty of exerting casual faith by bearing the name of God, while never in their lives intending to do his purpose. A father would not tolerate this kind of treatment by his son, and an employer would not allow it in his worker. Yet this is how the religious leaders in Malachi's day dared—and yes, how we today dare—to treat God!

Modern Christians need to have their lives spiritually recycled so they can experience God with more than their words—so they can experience God with their hearts and their total lives. Any person would hate to be ruled in contempt of court. It seems ironic that modern Christians are content to be in contempt of God for the casual faith they exhibit before God.

Questions for Thought and Discussion

1. What is your definition of God? Consider carefully to determine if there is a difference in your theoretical definition and your working definition.

2. How do you show reverence and respect for God?

3. Thoughtfully examine your life and cite specific instances in which your life does not demonstrate the religious words you utter.

4. In what ways does your verbal use of God's name indicate your feelings about him?

5. How would you describe prayer?

6. How can you have an honest, consistent, maturing prayer life?

7. Do you think people today honestly want to be forgiven in order to start afresh, or do they seek to be forgiven to continue to do as they please? Explain your answer.

Suggestions for Action

1. For a period of at least thirty days, set aside a daily time of prayer in which these specific aspects of prayer are included:

adoration,
thanksgiving,
dedication,
guidance,
intercession,
petition,
meditation,
confession,
forgiveness—both sought and offered.

It is helpful to use each of these elements of prayer, even if you divide your prayer time into a morning and an evening period. Hopefully at the end of these thirty days you will have found this experience so helpful in your Christian pilgrimage that you will make it a regular part of your daily life.

"By offering polluted bread upon my altar. And you say, 'How have we polluted it?' By thinking that the Lord's table may be despised. When you offer blind animals in sacrifice, is that no evil? . . . Oh, that there were one among you who would shut the doors, that you might not kindle fire upon my altar in vain! I have no pleasure in you, says the Lord of hosts, and I will not accept an offering from your hand. . . . But you profane it [my name] when you say that the Lord's table is polluted, and the food for it may be despised. *'What a weariness this is,' you say, and you sniff at me, says the Lord of hosts.* You bring what has been taken by violence or is lame or sick, and this you bring as your offering! Shall I accept that from your hand? says the Lord. Cursed be the cheat who has a male in his flock, and vows it, and yet sacrifices to the Lord what is blemished; for I am a great King, says the Lord of hosts, and my name is feared among the nations." (Mal. 1:7–14) RSV

3

Religious Boredom

Sir Thomas More, sixteenth-century chancellor of England, was about to be put to death by King Henry VIII. More had refused to betray an oath he had taken and deny his view of the church merely for the convenience of King Henry. With the urgency of saving his life, his family visited him in jail. There his daughter urged him to take a false oath, and thus be freed. She said: " 'God more regards the thoughts of the heart than the words of the mouth.' Or so you've always told me."[1] More agreed with his daughter that God was more concerned about internal substance than external appearance, but he would not, even for the sake of his life, use false, empty words. At the point of death, Sir Thomas More did not weary in being authentic in his attitudes, beliefs, words, and actions.

Many of the religious leaders of Malachi's day were not possessed with such authenticity and personal fortitude. Malachi said the religious leaders despised God's name by offering polluted food on God's altar. Perhaps they never stated so outwardly, but their attitudes and actions clearly indicated that the ritual of worship was for them a secondary function that required no great care on their part. Their actions shouted louder than their words that temple service was a most miserable job, which they performed only with contempt.

The "bread" brought to the altar basically meant food— meat or staple diet—offered to God. It was agreed that the people were required to sacrifice a first-rate animal—a one-year-old, spotless, healthy male (Deut. 15.19ff; Lev. 22:17–25). Therefore the priests were allowing offerings to be made that were improper on two accounts. First, the offerings were polluted because they were given with a hypocritical attitude. Secondly, they were improper because the animals were blemished and unfit for sacrifice. The priests should have reminded the people that they were not commanded or permitted to bring weak, diseased animals for sacrifice. But they did not tell them! The sacrificial system was based on the concept that the gift captured both the realization of the greatness of God and the consecration of the giver. To the ancient Hebrew blood was a symbol of life. In the covenant with God the sacrifice represented the individual. Thus, the animal was to be without spot and blemish, indicating the worshiper came before God with the impairments of life removed and with something as valuable as possible. Through their actions the religious leaders said that anything was good enough to be on God's table, God's altar.

The ironical thing about the people's offering God the leftovers of their table was that they thought they were getting by with it. They implied that in the long run their improper offerings made no difference to God. In his play *Cat on a Hot Tin Roof* Tennessee Williams focuses on the hypocrisy and dishonesty of the father, Big Daddy, and his son, Brick. Brick used a term to describe the lives they were living. That term was *mendacity*, or living lies.[2] As the play develops, both father and son realize the deceit that has existed in each of their lives, and Brick notes: "Mendacity is a system that we live in."[3]

The priests claimed to honor God, but deceit, mendacity, was the name of their game. Actually they despised God's name. So often when people enter a place designed for worship, they shift into neutral. They are neither for God nor against him. They are merely spectators. How we need to learn that when we truly worship God, we bring to him our proper attitude, offering, and communion—

the *best* we are and have,
    all we are and have!

With both the economic hard times and the religious so-
phistication that stressed that sacrifice was only a symbol,
the priests came to see no problem in making the sacrifice
from an animal of inferior quality. This completely over-
turned the highest ideals of the sacrificial system. Dr. J. J.
Owens, a Hebrew scholar, has made an interesting point. He
said there are two different attitudes present among those
who brought something other than the finest animals. The
owner said there was nothing wrong with bringing a blind
animal, for he was strong and robust. After all, others cannot always tell he is blind! Full of religious deceit, the owner
was the only one who knew, and he dishonestly claimed the
animal to be unblemished. This was a secret improper offering.

In the second place, the worshiper who swears "there is
nothing bad" about the animal that is lame or sick obviously
indicates both to God and to man that *he does not care!* It is
as though by whatever the worshiper called it, it was known
and accepted. Thus the religious people had been repeatedly
swearing falsely, bearing false witness straight into the teeth
of God. By our attitudes and actions some of us no longer
hide that we do not care what God or others think of our
superficial game of appearing religious.

There are a few nominal Christians today who would
openly declare something they have made or bought to be
their idol, their god. Yet, how many people inwardly dele-
gate to God only the castoffs of their love, concern, time,
attitude, money, or commitment? One of the apocryphal
books written shortly before the time of Christ, Wisdom of
Solomon, states:

> A skilled woodcutter may saw down a tree easy to han-
> dle and skillfully strip off all its bark,
> and then with pleasing workmanship make a useful
> vessel that serves life's needs,

and burn the castoff pieces of his work to prepare his
food and eat his fill.
But a castoff piece from among them, useful for
nothing, a stick crooked and full of knots,
he takes and carves with care in his leisure . . . .

                                    (Wisd. of Sol. 11-13b)

and makes of it an idol, his god! Are we not like that today?
Just like the people of Malachi's time, we have grown weary
in well-doing. We cut out from the pattern of "convenient
gods" the one we worship with our leftover resources and
energy. Often we are just going through a cultural motion.
Many of us have professed the name of Christ as Lord for
years, but we have not lived Christian lives. Some of us have
not been Christians in the first place, while others of us have
not committed ourselves completely to God in Jesus Christ.
We have only shoved our leftovers toward God! One writer
has asserted: "A religion fashioned out of second-rate material in our idle time hardly deserves the name; it is indeed
idolatry."[4]
   Would you dare be as indifferent to your boss as you are
to God? Would you give your superior as cheap and
thoughtless a gift as you give God? Of course not! You know
better than to give the one who signs your paycheck a
shoddy gift. You might lose your job, or at least you might
fail to receive that desired promotion. And so your boss is
more important than, is greater than, God! You give your
best quality and quantity to your earthly boss instead of
God.

   Oh, that there were one who would shut the doors [of
   the temple] and only let in worshippers. (Mal. 1:10a)

Malachi pled. Some active white church members say they
fear a person of another race might come into their sanctuary
and not have pure worship in mind. In keeping with Malachi's writing, a far graver concern should be the scores of ac-

tive white church members who enter the sanctuary weekly with no intent of worshiping God! What if there were a device to monitor your thoughts and emotions at the sanctuary door, and only genuine worshipers were admitted? Would you be allowed to enter? Worship is like a recipe. There are many elements that go into it before worship is completed. Improperly done, worship is always incomplete. Malachi was urging spiritual maturity among the people so they would gather in God's presence for the sole purpose of genuine worship.

Have you stopped to consider what God thinks about inflation? Though the people in Malachi's day were more prosperous than they had been in generations, often they claimed the high cost of living prevented their making their intended offering to God. Today our economy is highly inflated. Yet we have more than ever before. Many have the attitude of one lady who was overheard to say that although meat might be high, she would buy it, for her family was going to have meat. As the cost of attending professional sports events, organized entertainment, recreational clubs, and vacations goes higher and higher, most people continue their very same habits. And what gets slighted when they spend more and more of their income for more and more things? Their offering to God is the first area they cut back—in order to give their families what they want, mind you! From the pages of American church history, it used to be that withholding from God for one's own benefit was the exception. Now it seems that the improper offering to God has become more of a norm than an exception. We have accepted the idea that we give more today than last year for anything and everything—except our gifts to God.

Today we can substitute money for animal sacrifice. But God says he will not accept an offering that is given improperly. Some of us have tried to get around this fact by saying we give to the church to support the religious organization, to pay the charitable agency's bills, instead of saying we give our offering to God. For too many Christians there is little or

no surrender of self to God, even when we come to a place
set aside for corporate worship and we go through the motion of making an offering. We too frequently engage in an
external act without an internal personal experience. All the
commitment some feel is to a church's property or to some of
its members. Our attitudes, emotions, thoughts, words, and
actions are no different in the sanctuary than when we engage in the most ungodly act we commit. Indeed, we do not
genuinely worship God, for he makes no difference to us or
in us.

Surely Malachi shocked his people when God declared
through him that even though they had no specific training,
the non-Jewish nations were worshiping God in a more authentic manner than the Jews' careless priestly worship. The
Hebrew people had dishonored God with their indifferent,
religious boredom. God was declaring that he, his name, his
person was great, important, and essential to all people of all
times. The Hebrews were not so time conscious as we, and
there was no verb in God's declaration. The text literally
says:

My name great among the nations. (Mal. 1:11)

Not "was" great or "is" great or "shall be" great, but God's
name great—every time!

Malachi repeats in verse 13 what he stated earlier in verse
7, only he says more emphatically that the religious hierarchy was faulty. Of the whole religious life, from the sacrificial system to the corporate worship, the priests said:

"What a weariness this is!" (Mal. 1:13) RSV

Instead of considering their position of leadership as an
honor and a privilege, they saw it as a burden and a trouble.
They stuck up their noses at God with rebellious indifference
as though he were presumptuous in thinking he made any
difference or should be bothered by what the people were do-

ing. The religious boredom of the leaders was captured in the lives of the people as well.

> There passed a weary time. Each throat
> Was parched, and glazed each eye.
> A weary time! a weary time!
> How glazed each weary eye. . . .[5]

These words, written by Samuel Taylor Coleridge, actually describing the ancient mariner whose ship mysteriously went over the South Pole to the Pacific, seem to be descriptive of the weary look of many contemporary Christian worshipers. So often our faces reveal our minds are not actually encountering God; we are only physically present in a place where religion is being propagated.

Some people in Malachi's time dared to offer God what they had stolen from another. Through this action they were losing nothing themselves and they were attempting to make God a partner in their crime, thereby freeing themselves from punishment. Or if they did give of their own possessions, they gave only what they no longer could use or wanted to use. But Malachi reminds us this is both a wrong offering and it is given wrongly. It is not just what you do but the way you do it. It is not merely a payment to God but a giving of both the symbol of your life and your life itself to God that really counts. You can worship God and enjoy it, or you can worship and endure it. When the worshiper's, the giver's, attitude is improper, God does not accept the gift or the giver, regardless of the amount of the gift or the manipulative efforts of the giver. And yet we imply, we say, that God should accept us and bless us on the basis of our pious, self-righteous offering and worship. Do not be deceived any longer. Our mockery makes absolutely no impression on God!

A curse was placed on the one who during an illness or some other crisis had vowed a fine, expensive, healthy male animal—a purely voluntary sacrifice—but after recovery decided to give some weak animal that would not be much loss to him. He had the possessions to make the gift, but he did not give his best. Most of us today tend to make our gift to God out of what is left over rather than out of what we possess from the hand of God. The person Malachi cited "vowed," professed in public what he was promising, but then he offered another animal. He did not have the proper desire for or attitude of giving. He did not hold God with awe. How dare people make such offerings? It is better not to give at all than to profess and not live up to the profession.

How many times in the midst of crises have we pledged commitments to God and never lived up to them? Foxhole religion is not the worship of the True God. It is a gross perversion of worship. Surely it is more ungodly to serve God halfheartedly than to serve him not at all. It is better to ignore him completely than to presume one can trifle with him. We must commit our total beings to God. One outstanding Christian thinker and educator of a couple of generations ago was Dr. John R. Sampey, Old Testament professor, author, and seminary president. He had a private diary in a leather binding that had a lock and key. That diary was so private that not even his wife had access to it. He kept the key in the hidden pocket in his wallet. He confessed that when he prayed, he sought to withhold nothing from God. He opened and committed to God the prized key to his private diary so that he knowingly bared his whole being before God.

The genuine religious leader, Malachi stated, is the one who takes in God's knowledge and gives it out. Leading worship and teaching people of God are the most important and difficult tasks of professional and lay Christians alike. "To approach the altar carelessly and indifferently, to offer upon it anything less than the most perfect of sacrifice, is an offense in our day no less than in the days of Malachi. The Lord despises such service."[6] We who profess the name of God in Christ, whether or not we are elected leaders, need to determine if we have developed religious boredom through an improper way of living and worshiping. There is hope, joy, and forgiveness when we unreservedly commit our total being to God in Christ. Or we can go on being bored with our religion, pretending to be a Christian, and pushing the leftovers of our lives in the face of God!

Questions for Thought and Discussion

1. What is your attitude when you make an offering of money to God?
2. Do you ever feel that a large offering earns you special favor from God? If yes, why?
3. How do you interpret the view that the money you have given is symbolic of your life?
4. When do you decide what amount you will give God through your church?
5. What is the context for making an offering in your church? Do you feel the symbolism of offering your best to God through the money?
6. If money is only a symbol, in what ways do you seek to offer yourself to God other than by your money?
7. Have you ever had only pocket change left to make an offering to God in church? How did you feel then? How do you feel now?

Suggestions for Action

1. Decide on Monday the offering you will make the following Sunday and set it aside to be unused.
2. Seek at least one specific different way each week by which you can genuinely offer yourself to God.
3. As you place your offering in its envelope, pray consciously that God will take, use, and bless the gift.
4. Follow the course of action you choose for at least four weeks. If you are meeting in a group, share the results of this experience.

"By offering polluted bread upon my altar. And you say, 'How have we polluted it?' By thinking that the Lord's table may be despised."

"And now, O priests, this command is for you. If you will not listen, if you will not lay it to heart to give glory to my name, says the Lord of hosts, then I will send the curse upon you and I will curse your blessings; indeed I have already cursed them, because you do not lay it to heart. . . . But you have turned aside from the way; you have caused many to stumble by your instruction; you have corrupted the covenant of Levi, says the Lord of hosts, and so I make you despised and abased before all the people, inasmuch as you have not kept my ways but have shown partiality in your instruction." (Mal. 1:7; 2:1-2, 8-9) RSV

4

Indicting Dishonest Leaders

In the eight questions and answers Malachi used, none was as lengthy as the third one, beginning with chapter 1, verse 7. He was so emphatic in his indictment of dishonest religious leaders that this chapter is needed to conclude a two-part account of his statements. Additional verses of the text are printed on the opposite page to clarify the context.

Too often seminary and divinity-school students view what takes place in school as far removed from what will happen in a local church in the future. I spent six years in graduate studies, and I almost never came to grips with my need for developing depth relationships with others, strengthening my personal life, and establishing a reading program beyond what was required. I focused heavily then on academic matters, thinking that when I "got out," I would have the time and ability to develop the personal needs of my life.

The Beatles sang a popular song several years ago about the "nowhere" man. This character has no identity and no plans. He does not have a point of view, and he does not know where he is going. The song accurately concludes by asking if this nowhere man is not a symbol of many. Surely this song describes the malady of our times—the lack of purpose, direction, and real integrity in life. And may God forgive us, for not only is this true of the average man, but it also applies to those of us who call ourselves God's spokesmen!

Malachi continued the same rhetorical question raised in
1:7 throughout the first half of chapter 2. But in 2:1–9 he was
indicting the religious leaders for their dishonesty before
God. The priests of Malachi's day had the knowledge and
opportunity to exert a positive influence, but through their
lack of integrity they profaned God's name. They were so
wrapped up in religious practice that they delayed getting
their lives in order. They anticipated caring for their own
spiritual needs in the future. In his searching book, *To a
Dancing God*, Sam Keen warns us of the danger of always
living in anticipation, the fulfillment of which is never satisfied. Many of us have lived for the day we attained some
goal, but then we asked ourselves on its attainment, "Is that
all there is?" Perhaps you remember longing for the day you
would receive your driver's license, turn eighteen, graduate
from high school, complete college, become married, gain
your first full-time work, or complete your graduate work—
before you really started living. However, when you reached
that future plateau, life was still empty. The shocking reality
was that you had been imposing on yourself a self-made exile
from God, an exile that will continue with yet another "goal"
unless you break out of this pattern. We must learn not to be
dependent on the future in order to justify the present. The
healthy context for living is to gain simultaneously a sense of
awareness, memory, and anticipation. We need to live with
a vibrant present, a living past, and an open future.

Fortunately for me there was a break in my routine and
outlook before I finished graduate school. After five years as
a student minister, I spent my final year working in a depart-
ment store while completing my dissertation. During that
year I began to see how people in the world lived—not just
the "pagans," but also the members of local churches. In order to relate to fellow workers and customers with meaning,
I was forced to develop my personal spiritual life and at the
same time hone my professional tools. I say I was fortunate,
for I saw some classmates spend three to six years in aca-

demic studies and never come to grips with who they were, who God is, or how they were going to relate to people.

Preparation is important for every proclaimer of the Word of God—preparation in basic education and ongoing preparation to proclaim the Word each week. One of the great preachers in the first half of this century, Ernest Fremont Tittle, said: "Too many preachers are lying down on the job. Oh, to be sure, they are keeping busy, busy as bees, but not in the study. There they merely dabble and dawdle."[1] Many teachers, leaders, and ministers fail to use their time of preparation wisely so that their words and lives will make any real difference. Steinbeck's Elizabeth in *To a God Unknown*, says while standing at the altar being married: "Lord Jesus, make things easy for me because I am afraid. In all the time I've had to learn about myself, I have learned nothing. Be kind to me, Lord Jesus, at least until I learn what kind of thing I am."[2] Most of us have had in the past and have now in the present the kinds of professional resources and guidance to learn not what kind of "things" we are, but what kind of unique persons we are. Yet, we can waste all of our possibilities, obtain all kinds of professional credentials, and still have neither depth of personal commitment to Christ nor integrity as a healer of broken lives.

What is it that makes a person do an openly religious act without inner, genuine commitment—be it for a day or for a lifetime's work? Surely part of it is pressure from home or one's formative religious community. Another reason might be competition—living up to peer expectation. One aspect may be the success desire—wanting to get ahead and deciding that "Christian service" is about as good a way as any. This is especially true when one feels he can fulfill his humanitarian aspirations in a comfortable job while at the same time he is getting ahead in the eyes of the world. This pressure-competition-success desire can be drummed out time and time again in the years ahead if a man is dedicated only to seeking a "greater field of service."

The prophet Malachi spoke a sharp, penetrating, indicting word on this point (Mal. 2:1-9). Lest the religious leaders might think he was addressing the people of the land in general, Malachi said:

"And now, O priests, this command is for you." (Mal. 2:1)
RSV

Malachi is making unmistakably sure that the guilt of the ancient religious hierarchy was established. They were laboring with laxness, indifference, neglect of their teaching, and failure to use their minds properly. Contaminated as they were, the priests were wholly unfit for their official duty. In terms of letters, there is only a small difference between *ritual* and *spiritual*. But in terms of meaning there is a vast distinction. These religious leaders were given to ritual and were devoid of spiritual qualities.

Through Malachi God told those ancient ministers

if they will not listen,
if they will not lay it to heart,
if they will not intellectually, physically, and consciously see and accept their responsibility to
give glory and honor to God,
then he will curse them,
he has already cursed them, and
he will curse them again in the future!

This omnitemporal sense of God's message of judgment accurately pictures Old Testament prophecy. The prophets laid down broad principles of God's actions, and when people find those conditions again, they know what God will do, for he has done it before and he will do it again.

The point God was making with those religious leaders was that either they repent or they accept the judgment they chose for themselves. And judgment would surely come on them if they did not take God's Word seriously. He said he would rebuke their offerings, he would throw them into captivity if they acted like their forefathers, and he would put dung on their faces. And this was about the most downgrading treatment imaginable. The dung that was left in the courtyards by the animals used for sacrifice on the feast day was considered unclean and carried to some place and burned. Malachi likely meant that dung would be placed on the priests and the priests on the dung heaps. This kind of treatment would have been impossible while the people saw the priests as true men of God, as the true mediators between God and them. Dung would be used because of their dishonest actions.

Today the moral fiber of our land is weak, and many seem bent on developing an amoral land. It appears that God no longer actively figures in the lives of many persons—even some religious leaders! Some people become so wrapped up in collecting books they forget how to read them. Some people become so involved in the work of charitable organizations they fail to be kind themselves. And some people become so engrossed in religious activities that they lose sight of God's place in their lives.

Malachi reminded the priests of the covenant God established with Levi. Levi and his descendants were to fear, reverence, and worship God. In turn God would give them life and peace. Malachi told those religious leaders to look back to the rock from which they were hewn. Levi walked with God, not merely talked about him! Surely this remains one of the gravest temptations today for persons in places of religious leadership—just to use God talk and not know personal fellowship with God! Levi and the true priest knew unquestionable moral integrity, and they "helped many to find the way of life, others to return to it, and yet others to remain on this way."[3] The priests had the basic responsibility for informing the lay people what God expected of them. Unfortunately, the priests were not interpreting or living the Law adequately. Malachi concluded that they were the blind leading the blind in word and deed. As a result, the ancient leaders turned many persons away and caused others to stumble. They had forsaken God's intent, and they had lost the respect of the people.

The main problem Malachi saw was not a legalistic, ritualistic one. The priests were still going through all the motions. The problem was improper piety, improper attitude toward God. They knew God had created them, but they blamed God for the fact they were not showing love to each other and were mistreating one another. They accepted no personal responsibility for the fact they were partial and incomplete in what they taught of the Law, they profaned the sanctuary, they accepted inferior offerings, and then they wept and complained at the alter because the offerings were not accepted. Their dishonesty before God had become so ingrained in them that they had begun to believe the dishonest things they taught and lived.

Ancient priests, as well as modern teachers and ministers, were indicted for giving people what they wanted, telling them what they wanted to hear. The people had not been given the clear Word of God, even when it contained judgment and warning. These religious leaders had "watered down" their duties. This is not an advocation for rough insensitivity, but for sensitive, firm, courageous spokesmen. Surely one reason why so many cults and fundamentalist groups are popular today is that their leaders seem to speak with courage and authority.

In Malachi, as well as throughout the Bible, we can learn that we live spiritually on the installment plan—we live spiritually day by day—or we are not alive spiritually. A one-time commitment of ourselves to God is not enough. The initial decision to follow Christ in a church-related vocation is inadequate. An occasional seeking of God's will for our ministry is insufficient. God wants to be Lord of the whole world and of the whole man—beginning with and including you and me. If we are to know God's life and peace, we must be willing to give him the key to our innermost lives.

43

The description of Levi pictures an evangelist, a proclaimer of God's Good News, if there ever was one.

True instruction was in his mouth, and no wrong was found on his lips. He walked with me in peace and uprightness, and he turned many from iniquity. (Mal. 2:6) RSV

He took in the Word of God, and he put it out. God intended those ministers of Israel to be his spokesmen for the world. They failed him. God intends for us, his ministers, teachers, and leaders today, to practice the priesthood of believers—to interpret him to others; to assume our responsibility as disciples; to be participating, active ministers. Those ancient leaders turned aside from God's calling and thought more of themselves than of God. In the midst of perfunctory, hollow, empty, and lifeless religious practices, God always calls us back to our heritage, back to our Lord, back to his purpose for us. If we refuse, we are wrong and we will be punished.

We have a most difficult task. For we are very human and involved in the predicament of man, while at the same time we try to seek a solution to modern man's predicament. All too often, those who supposedly would turn the world upside down have not received Christ's strength and courage to stand up for him. Many of us easily and readily talk about the giants of the faith—the cost of Bonhoeffer's discipleship and the valor of a Bill Wallace in China. In spite of the words we say, we tend to trim our sails to go along with the prevailing winds. We act our roles cautiously, and still we complain about and question the Christian Church's impotence! One author writing on the ministry declared: "I think that your people have the right to claim that, by your way of living before their eyes, you should make plain the nature of the guided life."[4] If our ministry is not authentic, our manner of life becomes like that so skillfully described in a chapter entitled "Condemned to Sin Piously" in a book on the problems of the minister. Richard Baxter's admonition to seventeenth-century clergy still holds true: "Take heed of yourselves, lest you perish, while you call upon others to take heed of perishing; and lest you famish yourselves while you prepare their food."[5]

Lest we forget, the name of Christian ministry is "people." Whether the people among whom we serve are in a small rural church, a county-seat town church, or a city church, there are people with needs to whom God will send us with our abilities if we are willing to go. We need not think in terms of changing our site of ministry. The reference here is to touching the lives of the people in the community where we now reside and work. Too often we espouse personalism—personal salvation and discipline—while losing sight of others. In order to have a person-centered ministry we must know we are God's children and we must be able to affirm ourselves. A lot of people have not grasped what it is to be human or even more, how to do something worthwhile with their lives. People all over the face of the earth who think they are no good are going about trying to prove their goodness in order to earn God's love and acceptance. The good news is that Christ offers himself to those who know they are in need, not to those who think they are good.

Many talented persons are in a lot of turmoil in the ministry because they have never gotten their self-image in order. There are several choices a person has when he senses a loss of personal identity.

He might deal with the identity crisis he has become
    aware of,
he might consider his problem too great and withdraw
    from it,
he might ignore it altogether, or
he might want to deal with it but fail to dissolve his problem.

And then there are those persons who never become consciously aware of an identity problem. Surely the people who undertake the care of souls must gain for themselves self-understanding, personal knowledge, and awareness.

Otherwise, one might spend his life attempting to help others while never being genuine himself. This approach to life will be detrimental both to the minister and to his family. In addition, the failure of the minister to establish his own personhood will poison his relationship with his congregation.

A great many ministers have a low view of themselves. A man who does not consider himself worthy of being forgiven and accepted by himself or God finds it increasingly difficult to forgive and accept those among whom he ministers. Quite often a man will use the professional ministry to run away from his problems of personhood. And if the church becomes aware of the barrenness of his ministry, he might simply use the church as a scapegoat on which he projects responsibility for the difficulties of his ministry. And when such a dishonest man departs for "greener pastures" or "fields of greater service," he often leaves behind naïve, upset admirers whose own confused religious lives he so ably embodied and articulated.

Much has been said and even more written about the numerous problem areas of the minister's self-identity. Research has pinpointed the following outstanding difficulties:

> the minister's vocational motivation,
> his authority,
> his leadership,
> his hostility,
> his sexual adjustment,
> his ambition,
> his self-centeredness,
> his dependence on others for approval, and
> his loneliness.[6]

Different persons try to cope with their inner problems in various ways. The core of common efforts is expressed in these areas: accent on amiability by trying to be all things to all men, resort to sentimentality by constantly providing a soothing balm, addiction to activity, and surrender to the wrong authority—the people.[7]

The discovery of one's true personhood is significant. The four reactions just cited will drive a person deeper into his problems instead of freeing him from them. Unless a leader knows who he is, he may spend his life in lonely frustration, using and manipulating others for his self-satisfaction, never finding or fulfilling Christ's purpose for him. And it is ultimately in the encounter with Christ that one can recover his humanity and his sense of personhood. As is true with other helping professions, one of the unfortunate facts about the professional ministry is that the minister often becomes so busy serving others that his own emotional and spiritual needs may be neglected. The great preacher John Henry Jowett expressed this concept well in saying: "It is easier to be wise for others than to be it for oneself."[8]

When the minister has tended to his own spiritual life and has realistic expectations both of himself and of those among whom he works, he will be able to communicate authentic sensitivity and unquestioned integrity. The best preachers have been described as those who love themselves; who like, accept, and forgive themselves; and who realize their worth as creatures of God. These men have discovered the truth of Christ's statement that we are to love God completely and we are to love our neighbors as we love ourselves (Matt. 22:37-40). The minister who hates himself can never really love God or others.

There are several avenues to help the minister in discovering his own personhood and replace a poor self-image with a healthy one. Teachers, fellow ministers, family members, and friends may all be of help. Another avenue is to seek professional assistance just as we would consult a physician about bodily ailments. A third possibility is for the preacher himself to observe the surface manifestations of his deeper character and pursue their threadlike existence into the core of his being until he discovers their causes and relationships. In the best sense this is honest prayer. And it is in true prayer that a man can stand before God with absolutely no use of pretending and see himself as he really is before his Creator. Then as much as the minister himself is a whole person—able to relate to others in terms of their own personhood and able to be authentically committed in his religious devotion—he may be the instrument for the communication of truth to man.

There are many forces and urges within us, and unless our real self gets rootage and nurture, it will be pushed aside by the many negative selves clamoring for rule in our lives. It is a terrifying and disarming experience to give yourself over to the professional ministry and then to discover you have a disbelieving self, a doubting self, or an egotistical self that demands to be satisfied.

Would that we might learn to practice what we preach! Jesus often demonstrated his lesson first, then he taught it. He gave his finest lesson of service after he first took a towel to wash his disciples' feet (John 13:3ff). John Wycliffe was an eloquent preacher and profound teacher who demonstrated during the week what he planned to preach, and on Sunday he proclaimed to the people that which he had already lived before them. After Wycliffe preached, he then visited the sick, the aged, the poor, the blind, and the lame. And he nurtured them well.

The incident of Ananias and Sapphira in the early church is a graphic example of the personality of many professional churchmen—people who long for approval and thus pretend to be what they are not (Acts 4:32–5:12). Though others in the early church were giving all they had to the Christian commune, this couple was not demanded to do the same. However, when they pretended to be authentic in their Christian commitment, they were caught in their dishonesty. The disclosure of the lying self was more than they could take, and they fell dead. Unfortunately, for some churches in

our land, their ministers have not had such a direct encounter with the degree of integrity they possessed. Ananias
and Sapphira sacrificed their integrity, their state of being
complete, in order to make an impression and to gain acceptance. What a price they paid!

The novelist brings another truth when his character says:
"Oh, I know in my head how to be strong, but I can't learn to
do it."[9] Is this not where many of us are? We know that God
desires to enable us to be, but we have not given ourselves to
the task of learning to be today, as well as to become even
more tomorrow, Christ's minister. The life of integrity in the
minister possesses certain traits, including honesty,
straightforwardness, sincerity, and the courage to come to
terms with his own times of doubt. He is able to affirm his
humanity. He is humble and free from false pride, sham,
pretentiousness, and preoccupation with his own problems.
He has authentic hope, enthusiasm, and a healthy body—
mentally, physically, and spiritually. His commitment is
affirmed in that "he knows the God whose man he is."[10] The
minister of integrity can realize his preaching is report and
event. "Christ has found him. This is what he preaches; that
is why he preaches."[11]

Christ does not force us into a mold, but if we are going to
be authentic enablers who are equipped and functioning both
personally and professionally, we are going to have to
concentrate on our integrity now! Joseph, the main character
in To a God Unknown, took his own life in a misguided
attempt to help the people and the parched land. He
recognized and sought to know some higher power, but he
missed God—particularly because the local priest failed to
communicate with him at the place where he really ached.

Malachi declared to us that men stumble and fail to find
God when religious leaders are dishonest. Exile from yourself
and from God is always chosen. We need not go through life
as "nowhere men." It is possible to come home again—home
to self-realization, home to purpose in life, home to God's

abiding love in Jesus Christ. Would that we might be more like Levi, who internalized and proclaimed the truth of God's Word!

True instruction was in his mouth, and no wrong was found on his lips. He walked with me in peace and uprightness, and he turned many from iniquity. (Mal. 2:6) RSV

Those are beautiful words to be spoken of any follower of God in Christ—especially his chosen spokesman and leader.

Questions for Thought and Discussion

1. List the different types of dishonesty you are aware of among present or former leaders in your community and nation.

2. What is the difference in the integrity of public leaders who are Christians and those who are not?

3. In what ways are Christians dishonest with God?

4. Can you expect persons to be honest with their peers when they are not honest with God? Explain your response.

5. How have you come to grips with the lack of integrity and wholeness in your life? Are you dealing with self-identity problems in any of the four ways listed on page 45?

6. Consider the description of Levi in Mal. 2:6. Is this an accurate picture of the contemporary minister? Does it describe your life? Explain your answers.

7. Whom do you blame for the problems in your religious fellowship and in your life? Why?

Suggestions for Action

1. For at least two weeks keep a daily record of how much time you spend in reading and studying the Bible and how

much time you spend in other study to prepare you for your work. Weigh the hours of study against the 168 hours in a week and evaluate your priorities.

2. Set aside a period of time in which you can meditate and recall the feelings and motivating reasons which led you into professional Christian ministry. Write down your thoughts. If you have difficulty in evaluating what you have written, search out a competent counselor to assist you.

3. Review your preaching for the last six months to determine how often you have taught or preached what you felt the people expected to hear and were comfortable hearing and how often you preached or taught what you felt was God's Word for specific situations, regardless of how it might have been received.

"And this again you do. You cover the Lord's altar with tears, with weeping and groaning because he no longer regards the offering or accepts it with favor at your hand. *You ask, Why does he not? Because the Lord was witness to the covenant between you and the wife of your youth, to whom you have been faithless, though she is your companion and your wife by covenant.* Has not the one God made and sustained for us the spirit of life? And what does he desire? Godly offspring. So take heed to yourselves, and let none be faithless to the wife of his youth. 'For I hate divorce, says the Lord the God of Israel, and covering one's garment with violence, says the Lord of hosts.' So take heed to yourselves and do not be faithless." (Mal. 2:13–16) RSV

5

Breeding Ground for Breakup

A German playwright wrote an intriguing play about Andorra, a fictitious town in Protestant Europe. The play evolves from the reaction of the people to the schoolteacher's adopted son, Andri, who was said to be a Jew. The causes of the breakup of the teacher's family were not exclusively the prejudices of the people. The initial cause was the sexual immorality of the teacher while he was in another European country. Since he did not want to marry the woman who mothered his son, he ran off with him. He brought him back to his hometown as his adopted son. At that particular time Jews were accepted, even admired, by the teacher's people. Deceitfully he said he had rescued this infant "Jew" from a murderous crowd in a neighboring country. The townspeople considered the teacher a hero.

Later the teacher married and soon had a daughter born from that marriage. His illegitimate son, known as his adopted son, grew up and fell in love with his father's daughter. They had no idea they were related, much less half brother and sister! In the intense climax of the play the boy's mother, who was *not* a Jew, came to visit him and was murdered by the suspicious people of Andorra. In rather rapid succession the boy, Andri, who was not a Jew at all, was also killed by the prejudiced people who had now come to hate Jews. Then the teacher committed suicide. His daughter lost her mind from the shock of discovering her love was her half brother and then seeing him die. The man's wife was left alone.[1]

The teacher had lived with his lies for nearly twenty years, but the causes of the breakup of his family and his life had been growing during that time. He pretended there were no problems, yet they multiplied daily. Having spoken directly to the priests in the first nine verses of chapter 2, Malachi began looking at the sins of the laity. These sins were not acknowledged but were growing bigger daily. Malachi, the spokesman of God, pinpointed and condemned these acts. One was the commonplace marriage of Jews to wealthy, half-heathen neighbors. The other was the divorcing of their lawful Jewish wives, oftentimes for the purpose of establishing unholy alliances with pagan neighbors.

Malachi realized there were other grave sins, but he temporarily camped on the site of their marital unfaithfulness. God's intent for marriage has never been that it be a privately arranged affair for one's own personal convenience. Marriage is a very solemn covenant entered into in the presence of God. The obligations of marriage are not to be taken lightly (Ezek. 16:8ff). The Jews accepted the familiar truth of the Fatherhood of God and the corollary that all Jews were brothers and sisters. Malachi then asserted that every offense against that fraternal relationship—either marrying foreign women or divorcing Jewish wives—was a crime against God and against the sacred covenant that bound them to God as children to their Father. Early in the covenant relationship of God with his people, God had declared the Israelites were not to marry persons who were not of their own nation (Exod. 34:11–16; Deut. 7:1–5ff). The reason God had chosen a special people was not to exclude others. He sought to raise up a people who, in the midst of polytheism and idolatry, would nourish the true doctrine of God. The result of this authentic concept of God would be the proclamation of the love of God to all the ends of the earth.

We must not forget that the religion of the Hebrew people was something more than just what took place in their sanctuary. Modern Christians are often oriented to the concept that what happens in the church's buildings comprises the sum total of their religious experience. Most of the religious learning in Malachi's day took place in the Jewish home. The majority of the worship occurred in the home. The fantastic amount of memorization of Scripture and religious tradition transpired in the home. A woman—a wife and a mother—who knew nothing about the worship of the One True God would basically be a corruption, a distortion, or a literal destruction of the worship of God in the home! That same woman would also successfully seek to inject into the Jewish home the worship of her pagan god. Besides the destruction of the worship of God in the home, it was improper for a pagan woman to enter the Temple where she would profane the sanctuary (Mal. 2:11).

The prophet pronounced a curse on those who felt community ties and loyalties so slightly that they would be involved in mixed marriages. They were to be excommunicated from Judea. People who broke the covenant with God and their fellowmen were to be deprived of access to the law court and the Temple. The Jewish religion was embodied in the total realm of their lives. It was a serious thing to deny their religion and break the established covenant.

Divorcing of Jewish wives had become so prevalent in Malachi's day that he focused on it as a major evil. Divorce was a breaking of the marital covenant made before God and the Jewish community. It also broke the covenant that had been established between God and the Hebrew people. Divorce almost always worked a great hardship on the woman who was set aside. She usually had to resort to prostitution in the streets. Divorce likely took place to allow the Jew to marry a pagan wife, or at least a younger, more attractive Jewish wife.

Some have interpreted Malachi's description of tears on the altar to be those of divorced women (Mal. 2:13). More likely the tears came from those who had committed treacherous deeds and then cried because God did not accept their ceremonial acts of worship. They went to their place of worship with no thought of forsaking their sins, and then they had the nerve to complain when God did not make life fulfilling for them! Using the classic question, Malachi inquired:

> *"You ask, 'Why does he not?' "*

His response was:

> *"Because the Lord was witness to the covenant between you and the wife of your youth, to whom you have been faithless, though she is your companion and your wife by covenant."* (Mal. 2:14) RSV

God never looks with favor on the hypocrites who form and then break a covenant—with a marriage partner as well as with God—especially when they have the power to keep their covenant, their agreement.

Malachi's declaration that God hates divorce (Mal. 2:16a) is recorded nowhere else in the Old Testament. At this point he was very close to what Jesus said a few centuries later (Mark 10:2-9; Matt. 5:32, 19:3ff). He said the people were to discontinue divorce because God hated their conduct and they were covering themselves with sin. The reference to covering with sin or violence probably means an act that is unjust or violent toward one's wife or toward the marital relationship.

The home, the private lives, and the religion of the Hebrew people were breaking up because of marriage outside their religion and because of divorce. This summation of what developed over several centuries gives us cause to examine the bases of breakup in twentieth-century homes. Numerous factors present before a marriage largely influence the future of that relationship. One grave obstacle to successful marriage is the lack of adult guidance in our society. A lot of attention and counsel are given to the choice of school and vocation. But the main responsibility is left to young people to interpret by themselves their plans and feelings about making marriage last a lifetime. This situation is not altogether bad, but it is nonetheless a grave responsibility, often undertaken by people just reaching adulthood.

Many people have a rather casual attitude toward marriage, whether or not they are mature or immature socially and physically. Some want their marriages to be "successful," but they may seem unconcerned if it does not last for a lifetime. They will "try it for a while" and see if they "like it." And if they do not like the marriage, there appears to be no anxiety about dissolving it. Some of the most immature and soluble relationships are those established mainly on physical attraction. After the Hollywood romanticism has evaporated in the midst of struggling with the difficulties of life, most of these marriages soon go under.

Probably the gravest premarital problem is that many couples have no sense of the biblical concept of marriage as a covenant established before God and man. On the one hand, there is a lot of premarital sex play based on physical excitement. On the other hand, there is no genuine sense of pledge of fidelity on the part of husband and wife to each other. Often a couple seem not to realize there is a price to pay in order to unite two lives into one. Many women are unready to set aside opportunities for career advancement and personal independence in order to accept the routine duties of bearing and rearing children. Numerous men are unwilling to use their financial resources wisely for the family, nor do they take care to share with the family some of the attention focused exclusively on their work. The family does deserve an expenditure of time as well as money.

In their helpful book *The Recovery of Family Life* Dr. and Mrs. Elton Trueblood have spelled out three important features of the Christian concept of marriage. One, it is a covenant of commitment, not merely a legal contract. The family relationship is accepted as unconditional, not as a trial period. Two, marriage is a public, not a private, institution. Marriage does contribute to or take from society. Three, marriage involves the free acceptance of a bond—a disciplined limit to self-expression.[2]

After marriage one big cause of breakup is the very same thing Malachi witnessed: husband and wife not being one in God. Many couples have established a "good" life for themselves, but they leave no room for individual or family worship of God. The strongest home is based on a shared relationship with God. No two people can fulfill all the needs of each other. Their ultimate fulfillment comes through their common concern and their mutual devotion to God. For every home that has broken up where husband and wife were genuine, maturing Christians there have been several dozen breakups in homes of nominal Christians or homes of people who had no concern for God.

Infidelity causes many marriages to crumble. Why does it happen? Some marriage partners are unfaithful only mentally for a time, but then it becomes physical also. Some people practice extramarital sex to boost their ego, to convince themselves they are still young and vivacious. Others are possessed with lust or the desire to conquer or be accepted. Sometimes a person is flattered that someone is interested in them. Almost all of these factors figured in King David's seduction of Bathsheba. A careful study of that story reveals that both of them played a part in their illicit affair. David first saw her when he was walking along his roof, a common practice, and she was taking her bath in plain sight (2 Sam. 11:2–5)!

A great many people are unfaithful because of their low self-esteem or their lack of commitment to their marriage partner. There was a time when infidelity occurred among those who failed to do what they knew they should. Now many have lost the sense of meaning of the family, and our "basic failure is not the failure to live up to the standard that is accepted, but rather the failure to keep the standard clear!"[3] We would do well to remember that we are not created sexual animals to run about doing what "feels natural." God created male and female to enable two people to become one in the fullest and most complete sense, of which sex is only a part (Matt. 19:6–9).

A main factor in the breaking up of marriages is that people simply drift apart. Instead of the two being one, they co-exist in the same house, each going a separate way. Married partners, and a family, can experience a relationship of intimacy, understanding, support, love, and concern. Yet, we find "the constricting pressures of intimacy a heavy burden. We have been trained for a highly individualized way of life—winning our place through the things we do. . . . We need intimacy. We are not sure that we can live with it."[4].

We seldom do anything together as families. Husband, wife, and children spend most of their waking hours going in as many different directions as there are people or, seemingly, *more* directions than people! Some families meet only for boring meals or arguments about money. Frequently in this type of home the outer shell of marriage is maintained only "for the sake of the children." The heart has gone out of the marriage. Only an illusion is created when all the family sleeps under the same roof. Other than sporadic outbreaks of adultery, most couples conceal very well from the world that their marriage is empty and dead. There is no love, no genuine relationship. This is the way intimacy is usually lost in a marriage—it just slips away when the couple no longer desire it or work for it. Suddenly a couple wake up in the middle of their lives with no love, no marriage! This is the marriage described as two people who

> are lonely together because they have not continued to work at their relationship. . . . It's more than simply *doing* things together, although that's important. It's *being* together both physically and emotionally, sharing in

each other's world of feelings, hopes, anxieties, and dreams, that keeps in good repair the bridge that joins two persons. It's this that makes love grow and flower.[5]

Howard and Charlotte Clinebell write in their book *The Intimate Marriage*, that other than during the time of engagement and the very early years of marriage, intimacy is needed during the middle years of life more than at any other point. At whatever stage your marriage may be, if you have grown or are growing apart from your mate, now is the time to work to see if you can rescue your marriage. If your marriage is about empty, about to break up, do not work alone. Seek the assistance of your minister or a marriage counselor. You can learn greater intimacy as a couple

when you are willing to risk more openness with each other,
when you show more deeply that you care for each other,
when you become more understanding of each other, and
when you develop a genuine commitment of trust and love.

Some marriages break up because they slip into coexistence. Others break up because they were never anything more than dreams. Arthur Miller describes Willie Loman as just such a make-believe husband/father in his play *Death of a Salesman*. Willie had such dreams of success that he rejected the need to establish intimacy with his family. He transferred them into his world of make-believe. He could not tolerate anything about them that did not conform to his dreams. His imaginary picture of his family tended to bolster the dream he had for himself. After his suicide his son, Biff, says of him: "He never knew who he was."[6] Ironically, Willie Loman could have done well enough as a salesman and as the head of his family had he once escaped from his imaginary world. But then, some of us do not want to escape, do we?

Often divorce is used for one's selfish convenience. King Henry VIII had prevailed upon the pope to dispense with the sixteenth-century Christian law that prohibited a man from marrying his brother's widow. Henry then married Catherine of Spain, the widow of his late brother, Arthur. Later Henry wanted out of the marriage because it had provided no male heirs. When the pope and Chancellor Sir Thomas More stood in the way of a divorce that would allow Henry to marry Anne Boleyn, Henry had More executed, and he passed the Act of Supremacy, which made him head of the Church of England, free of papal Rome. King Henry was determined to have a divorce so he could have his own way.

Given the set of circumstances, divorce may seem to be the only way to salvage anything of two lives, much less a family, that have broken in two. Divorce is always failure, and since we are human, divorce will always be with us. It is not an unpardonable sin. Still, we should not approach marriage or be in marriage expecting divorce as the outcome. We should discourage divorce and seek legislation to prevent its being an easy alternative. And we should stress the willing acceptance of the covenantal bond of marriage.

There is one final truth underlying the figure of the marital relationship in Malachi. He used the one word, marriage, to start his listeners thinking about something else. One word said two things. Malachi said that a person's relationship with humanity revealed something about his relationship with God. The Jewish people were forsaking the True God, the God of earlier days, for a new marriage partner, a new god, a new participant in the covenant. The first evidence of skepticism toward God was the neglect of Temple worship. Now the spirit of indifference was seen in the dying down of enthusiasm for maintaining a distinct existence as the people of God. The mixed marriages and divorces would not have taken place if the people had been fully conscious of their relationship with God. Since their faith in God was declining, they forgot their duties to him and to each other, and they carried on as they well pleased!

When they were in trouble, the people cried to God to be delivered. As soon as he delivered them, they forgot him again. Over and over they did the same thing. Now they were on the altar again, covering it with tears; they thought if they used the right formula, cried enough tears, and acted religious enough, God would get them out of difficulty another time.

Is this the same kind of song and dance we frequently perform today? We live as we please, and then we go through a religious formula, a prescribed ritual, and plead for God to make life good and easy for us. If we go before God weeping, we must be sure our hearts are open to be renewed by him. We can grow in our relationship to God and in our relationship to each other through the love, strength, and mercy of God in Christ Jesus. We can establish the kind of relationship that will not break up if we desire it strongly enough.

But if we honestly want this kind of life of intimacy with God and with our marriage partner, we have to be willing to see the potential causes of breakup within ourselves. And then we must be willing to work—on ourselves.

Questions for Thought and Discussion

1. Describe the impact you feel two genuine, practicing Christian parents can have on the religious development of their children.

2. Mental infidelity in marriage is wrong and frequently leads to physical infidelity. Do you agree? Why or why not?

3. Describe the various persons affected as a consequence of divorce.

4. Do you agree with the statement made on page 61 that "a person's relationship with humanity revealed something

about his relationship with God"? Why or why not?

5. Do you feel people think they can win God's favor and love through pretentious religious acts? Explain your answer.

Suggestions for Action

1. If you have not already done so, establish a time of worship, of study, of family religious discussion in your home. Set aside ten to fifteen minutes a day for a month's trial period.

2. Try for at least a week to work on your relationships with others—especially those in your immediate family. Listen actively to what they say verbally and nonverbally. Consider thoughtfully how your response could be interpreted. Seek to affirm others instead of tearing them down.

3. If your marriage is growing weak—and especially if separation or divorce is potentially near—seek a competent counselor this week to assist you in working through your marital problems.

4. For a brief, healthy reading assignment read Paul Tournier's *To Understand Each Other* (Atlanta, Ga.: John Knox Press, 1974).

5. For a more intense assignment read and work through as a couple Clinebell's *The Intimate Marriage.*

6. Schedule at least one special evening with your spouse each week for a month. If it cannot be an evening out together, consider going out for breakfast or lunch—but have a time just for the two of you to be together and talk.

7. For at least a month set aside one evening a week to be together as a family. Put this on the top of your priorities of time.

8. Set aside a period of quiet, personal time in which you can reexamine your commitment to God in Christ. Determine if you have wandered from your original covenant and allowed other gods to supersede God's rightful place in your life.

"You have wearied the Lord with your words. Yet you say, 'How have we wearied him?' By saying, 'Every one who does evil is good in the sight of the Lord, and he delights in them.' Or by asking, 'Where is the God of justice?'

"Behold, I send my messenger to prepare the way before me, and the Lord whom you seek will suddenly come to his temple; the messenger of the covenant in whom you delight, behold, he is coming, says the Lord of hosts. But who can endure the day of his coming, and who can stand when he appears?

"For he is like a refiner's fire and like fuller's soap; he will sit as a refiner and purifier of silver, and he will purify the sons of Levi and refine them like gold and silver, till they present right offerings to the Lord. Then the offering of Judah and Jerusalem will be pleasing to the Lord as in the days of old and as in former years.

"Then I will draw near to you for judgment; I will be a swift witness against the sorcerers, against the adulterers, against those who swear falsely, against those who oppress the hireling in his wages, the widow and the orphan, against those who thrust aside the sojourner, and do not fear me, says the Lord of hosts.

"For I the Lord do not change; therefore you, O sons of Jacob, are not consumed." (Mal. 2:17–3:6) RSV

6

Judgment Is for Real

The Jewish people experienced one of the gravest times of persecution during the second century before Christ. Judea had lived under the descendants of first one Greek general and then another since Alexander the Great conquered the Mediterranean world.[1] Early in the second century first subtle, then overt, steps were taken to bury the Jewish religion beneath the Greek religion. Initially the Jews only had to structure their religion in order not to offend the Greek god Zeus. Then they were told they had to acknowledge that Zeus had become incarnate in the Greek ruler, Antiochus Epiphanes IV.

> They had to pay homage to this ruler.
> They had to cease circumcising their sons.
> They had to sacrifice a swine on the altar to Zeus.
> They had to kiss the statue of Antiochus.

James Michener's historical-fictional novel *The Source* describes why one group of Jewish people went along with this Greek rule for a quarter of a century.[2] The local Greek ruler persuaded the local Jewish leader, Jehubabel, that the Jewish religion would not be overridden. It was ironic that Jehubabel, whose name literally meant "Yahweh is in Babylon," was the religious leader. He came to be in that position for two strange reasons. One was because he lived next door to the synagogue, and the other was due to the fact that he had read the Jewish classics. He had forgotten what the learned Jewish scholars had written, but he did remember several dozen pithy sayings from the centuries of Jewish tradition. Jehubabel was full of words and sayings that sounded deep and involved, although most often they meant nothing to the situation at hand. Jehubabel was so caught up with his Jewish proverbs that he did not see the essential conflict in the initial order to worship both Antiochus Epiphanes in the temple to Zeus and Yahweh God in the synagogue.

The Greek governor disliked working with his Jewish counterpart. Jehubabel always took refuge in a constant barrage of pithy statements when intellectual problems needed to be faced. The Greek wished his Jewish colleague would forget his sayings and face the reality at hand. Jehubabel's lack of perception led to the weakening and destruction of his people. And his preoccupation with religious sayings drove his son from him. Communication was impossible between the two of them because Jehubabel was so insulated within the comforting shelter of endless words.

Tragedy overcame the Jewish people and Jehubabel's family when in anger Jehubabel killed his son, who had become a converted Greek. The outcome included the Jewish people's fleeing from their homes, a prelude to the Maccabean revolution against the Greek ruler. Novelist Michener indicted Jehubabel by saying that only Antiochus Epiphanes's appearance prevented Jehubabel's living out a bland life, spouting forth trivial adages.

It is saddening to read what took place in the life of this so-called religious leader and his family, as well as in the life of the Jewish community. Yet this situation was the outgrowth of what Malachi had described over two centuries earlier (Mal. 2:17–3:6). The people who were supposedly religious were only filled with empty words, words that caused God to say he was weary. All of us have been in a situation where we sat impatiently, waiting for a talkative person, a "windbag," to wind down, wondering if we could hold still until that person finished. How weary we became! Can you not hear God as he declared to the people of Malachi's day that he was tired of hearing the endless repetition of words? Indifferently mouthed words had become the sum total of the religious life of the people.

The people responded to Malachi's assertion that God was simply worn out with their talking by asking:

"How have we wearied him?" (Mal. 2:17b) RSV

Their question was slanted not only to justify themselves for their sin, but also to place the blame for their problems on God. Malachi told them they wearied God by saying God's influence was benefiting the wicked instead of the righteous and by saying God was not going to judge—either those they called wicked or the Jewish people themselves. Since the non-Jewish nobles were prosperous and the neighboring nations were stronger than they, the Jewish people said the moral order of the world was distorted. The evildoers seemed to be the ones God considered good! "When evil seems to flourish unrestrained, when good men feel no apparent worth in worship and are content to offer less than their very best to God, the reality of God's judgment is always questioned."[3]

The Jewish people had been through many trying times in the preceding thousand years. They had seen their cities destroyed many times, and they had been carried away captive to foreign lands. Out of one side of their mouths they were saying God had stopped blessing the "good" people. Out of the other side of their mouths they were implying that after all they had been through, especially since they were God's chosen people, God would not judge or punish them anymore. And is this not like the attitude of many Americans today? More than one radio program gives false propaganda to people. Some teach that Britain and the United States are the lost tribes of Judah, special countries in

the entire world in the sight of God. This whole theory is un-
sound biblically. In Malachi's day all the Israelites were
reunited. But the Hollywood-commentator style of some
religious broadcasters has given many persons a distorted
concept of America. An additional injustice has been done
when views of God's judgment and the end of the world re-
sound with a harsh note of destruction but with no concern
for salvation of those outside the United States and Britain.[4]
This is not what God's justice and judgment are all about!

Malachi's view of judgment involved two acts. First a
messenger would purify the Temple and the priestly order.
Then the Lord himself could come to the Temple, where he
would judge the people according to their lives. In the
analogy of the ancient king and his palace God was described
as a king and the Temple his palace. He would not come into
the Temple until it was set in order. His messenger, his
forerunner, would correct the Temple abuses (Mal. 1:6–2:9).
Once again worship could be done with dignity and
sincerity.

How the people were longing for "that day," just "one
day" in the presence of the Lord with everything as it should
be! The day of the Lord's coming, the "day of Yahweh," had
been long awaited by distressed people. They tended to see
the day of God's coming as a time of prosperity and
deliverance from oppression and their enemies. Malachi
declared they would be surprised in what that "one day"
would reveal. At his coming none could endure the day of
God. No one would be able to stand in his presence.

Malachi saw God's judgment, God's coming, to be
primarily for the purpose of cleansing or purifying, rather
than destroying. He used two well-known trades to indicate
God's purpose: the refining of gold and the cleansing of
clothes—the refiner's fire and the fuller's soap. The cleansing
and purification would continue until the right offerings
were presented to God. This concept of God's judgment is
expressed in both the Old and the New Testaments. For the

faithful, the authentic people of God, there would be purification. For the godless, those who willfully choose to reject God's love, this manifestation of God would mean destruction of the impurities that cannot be cleansed.

New England's far-reaching spiritual movement of the mid-eighteenth century was considered to have been touched off by a sermon preached by Jonathan Edwards. This was not a typical sermon of Edwards. His description of the reality of judgment under the title "Sinners in the Hands of an Angry God" caused a Great Awakening for many. Some have accused Edwards of using "scare tactics" to prompt public response. His intent seems to have been that of declaring that the only thing that saves a person from hell is God's grace and love. God has no obligation to save a person. And when one rejects God and in evil struggles to get away from God, it is as though he is sliding around on slippery ground at the edge of a great hole. When one pushes God away, when he pulls his hand and his life out of the hand of God, he plunges to destruction. God's judgment is for real. It is the other side of his love. To reject his love, his mercy, his grace, and his salvation is but to ask for his judgment.

Edwards noted that almost no one would want to be punished for his sins. Thus the sinner tries to figure out a means of escape. All the while he is calculating, he is rejecting the Lordship of God and is remaining evil. Edwards preached: "Almost every natural man that hears of hell, flatters himself that he shall escape it; he depends upon himself for his own security, he flatters himself that he contrives well for himself, and that his schemes will not fail." Although the people in Edwards's day were accustomed to hearing that only few were to be saved, "each one imagines that he lays out matters better for his own escape than others have done: he does not intend to come to that place of torment; he says within himself, that he intends to take care that shall be effectual, and to order matters so for himself as not to fail."[5]

The contemporary person who longs for a "day of the

Lord" is not thinking so much about his own sins being judged as he is anticipating his enemies being judged. We want to be blessed, not punished. We most often simultaneously request our own benefits while asking for the punishment of others. Malachi emphasized that the Lord is coming, though his judgment may not be to the people's liking. God knows the facts about the people and will not need to search for more evidence before judging them. Since God is both judge and witness, judgment can be promptly and properly executed.

Malachi was no mere ritualist. He recognized the sins against humanity that were being committed. "Looking more deeply into the human heart than some of his predecessors, he saw that contempt for the symbols of religion may be not a sign of spiritual emancipation, but the symptom of a profound contempt for religion and morality itself."[6] Malachi saw the sins against one's fellow man in the focus of God's concern. God's justice will be given out to all who have mistreated their fellow man. Those who use all the proper-sounding words but do not have godly love for others cause God to be weary. His mercy will cease for those who instead of loving their neighbors use only meaningless words while they

> trick the innocent
> commit adultery
> behave dishonestly
> cheat workers
> take advantage of widows and orphans
> brush aside the stranger or foreigner
> and fail to have due respect and awe for God
>
> (Mal. 3:5)

Mosaic law warned against all these wrongs, and they will not be overlooked by God.

This Word of God through Malachi offers the contemporary person insight for renewal. Too many nominal Christians' lives are filled with the sins of covetousness and exploitation, the sins of a humanity indifferent to the conditions that breed misery, poverty, and sickness. We need to realize that much of the disbelief of non-Christians is due to the character and performance of the Christian laity. These contemporary religious persons frequently pretend to possess all kinds of Christian experiences and graces while lacking the fundamental virtues that are both admitted and practiced by the non-Christian person. This very act of professing Christians—spineless words—causes religion to be in disrepute with the average non-Christian. "They see men and women claiming to be Christians, talking about faith and grace, sanctification and regeneration, who yet somehow do not seem to incorporate in their moral make-up certain elementary virtues of simple honesty, courage, generosity and loyalty which every decent man is supposed to possess."[7]

The reality of God's judgment is captured in the understanding that we need not perceive the mysteries of life, of suffering, of illness, and of death to determine that God is just and he will judge all men. The day of reckoning will come when God will confront all of us with whether we chose to accept his love, forgiveness, restoration, and Abundant Life, or we chose to reject his good gifts.

What makes us think—in spite of our moral goodness, our acquisitions, our faithful church attendance, and our generosity with others—that we are exempt from God's judgment? Those of us who are in Christ can be assured the future is in God's hands. We do not have to be threatened by the seeming success of godless financial giants in the land. Our wealth, our security, our joy, and our life are ultimately to be found only in the presence of God, the Great God, who offer us the best of his grace now and the assurance of his blessings throughout endless ages. God's call to us who are his people is the summons to be cleansed of our vain religious language and our immorality toward each other.

Harvard church historian George La Piana has said there are three stages every religious movement passes through— ethical, theological, and aesthetic. The beginning of the movement is based on moral reform. A reflective time of formulating faith and practice follows. Finally there is elaboration in terms of the beauty of the buildings and the ritual of worship. "The last of these stages marks a point of intellectual arrest and often of incipient moral decay. The movement must then be born again in a fresh formation, primarily moral in its intention."[8]

Perhaps modern Christians have been snagged on a preoccupation for church property, a concern that has replaced interest in moral affairs. Attention to proper doctrine, attractive buildings, and significant worship is important. Yet all the ecclesiastical property, all of the right statements, and all of the religious proverbs become nothing more than droning words that weary God when our faith ceases to be morally earnest.

God challenges us to be wise, honest, and courageous enough to quit hiding behind the accusation that he is unjust or that we are so good we will not have to answer for our willful rejection of him or abuse of our fellowman. God will judge us in light of what we are doing today. Now is the time to act on this prophetic insight by ceasing our attempt to deceive both God and others. We can realize the reality of God's judgment or continue to fool ourselves—the choice is ours.

Questions for Thought and Discussion

1. What kind of reaction do you have when people talk big but never implement their words into their living?

2. What contemporary religious life-styles do you feel cause God to be weary?

3. In light of Malachi's writing, how would you define the judgment of God?

4. Does God deal with all people with equal justice? Explain.

5. Do you feel your religious professions will merit you special favor from God? Explain.

6. How can you justify desiring blessings for yourself while asking for punishment for others?

7. Is there equal emphasis in your church on moral uprightness as there is on building programs?

8. In the quotation on page 70, the writer declares that "contempt for the symbols of religion may not be a sign of spiritual emancipation, but the symptom of a profound contempt for religion and morality itself." Do you agree or disagree that this statement is accurate for today? Explain.

Suggestions for Action

1. Reread Bennett's quotation on page 67 and write your evaluation of this statement. If you are doing this study in a group, share what you have written.

2. Make a list of things you might do differently in order to change your behavior to match your religious words. Include in your consideration of areas that need improvement the list on page 70. Note specific people with whom you want your actions changed. Evaluate your effort at the conclusion of two weeks.

3. If you feel there is inadequate emphasis on moral uprightness in your church or religious group, ask permission to speak to a group or to church leaders or to a church business meeting. Request that a serious study be done to seek ways of shifting the emphasis of the religious body from buildings to living for God lives that are morally upright.

"From the days of your fathers you have turned aside from my statutes and have not kept them. Return to me, and I will return to you, says the Lord of hosts. But you say, 'How shall we return?'" (Mal. 3:7)

7

The Tricks Pride Plays

The story is told of a monk from a Christian order who explained the distinctive quality of his group in these words: "When it comes to good works, we don't match the Benedictines; as to preaching, we are not in a class with the Dominicans; the Jesuits are way ahead of us in learning; but in the matter of humility, we are tops."[1] This facetious description pinpoints a grave problem. That problem is pride, the false egoism that inflates us to the point others find it difficult to live with us and we find it impossible to relate properly to God. Pride has many shades of meaning. It can indicate open-eyed realization of one's God-given capacities, skills, and worth. Pride is also commonly displayed as undue self-esteem, complacency, arrogance, or boasting.

An unhealthy pride rots man's personality at its core. More than one person has declared that other sins, such as greed, anger, gluttony, and unfaithfulness, are mere fleabites when compared with pride. Pride is not only the most subtle and destructive sin, but it also is the root of most other sins, such as envy, anger, sloth, lust, and gluttony. Pride leads to injustice, which is a major source of evil. Pride may lay behind drunkenness, which gives a person a sense of power normally denied him in life. Sexual acts may be used to dominate another person. Envy and vanity have the rather obvious flavor of pride. And greed is pride's servant, giving one the opportunity for displaying his superiority over others.

Malachi was struggling to crack a hole in the spiritual pride of the people to whom he prophesied. Those people implied the trouble was rooted in a change in God's attitude. They boldly claimed there was nothing wrong with them. Malachi clearly answered that assertion by declaring there was no change in the character of God, but there was a change in the people's attitude to him (Mal. 3:6, which is an answer to 2:17). God's attitude toward evil is always the same. His love and compassion also abide unchangeable. He is not fickle toward man the way man is toward him.

As long as can be remembered, the covenant people had rebelled against Yahweh God (Mal. 3:7). The ordinances, statutes, and will of God—oral or written, expounded by prophet or priest—the people had disregarded them all. The people's disobedience and absence of faith made them unable to perceive the presence of God. Their turning aside from God made them closed and unresponsive to God's revelation and blessing.

Shortly after the Israelites had escaped the Egyptian bondage God said to them through Moses:

> "You have seen what I did to the Egyptians, and how I bore you on eagles' wings and brought you to myself. Now therefore, if you will obey my voice and keep my covenant, you shall be my own possession among all peoples; for all the earth is mine, and you shall be to me a kingdom of priests and a holy nation. These are the words which you shall speak to the children of Israel."
>
> So Moses came and called the elders of the people, and set before them all these words which the Lord had commanded him. And all the people answered together and said, "All that the Lord has spoken we will do."
>
> (Exod 19:4–8a) RSV

The people, both then and repeatedly after that occasion, promised their love and obedience to God in the covenantly relationship. Yet time and again they failed to live up to their word. They did not maintain God's law, God's expectation, and God's ordinance. The Hebrew word for "ordinance" literally means a boundary or prescribed limit. Malachi was giving a picture of the people making a false turn while the true way was very clearly marked. "Israel had repeatedly gone beyond the boundaries or limits prescribed by her covenant God. But in spite of her faithlessness, Yahweh had remained faithful and continued to be merciful, gracious, slow to anger, and abounding in steadfast love and faithfulness."[2]

Malachi declared that if the people would return to God, the fulness of his presence and blessing would return to them. God loved them as he had always loved them in the past. The need was for them to repent. The issue was Israel's *faithlessness* versus God's *faithfulness*. The people were complaining that God had forsaken them. The truth was they had forsaken and ignored God! Their returning to God was not just their turning in a particular direction, but their retracing their steps. They had to return to the road from which they had wandered. Repentance involved a change of attitude. For the Hebrew mind that attitude had to be manifested in action.

It is with a deep sense of awe, gratitude, and humility that I realize God's initial message to us is always a call to repentance, not a weighty pronouncement of final judgment. Just as he did to Israel, God lovingly invites us to return to his way and walk with him. He says:

"Return to me,"

in love and obedience,

"and I will return to you"

in loving-kindness and mercy (Mal. 3:7b; Joel 2:12–14; Hos. 14:1). The prophet was not saying that God withholds judgment forever, but that at the present time he still extends his mercy. There is opportunity for us to confess our sins and repent. The day of God's judgment is certain, though the day has not been dated for us. Now is the time for repentance and renewal.

To this very pointed description of their spiritual need the people replied to Malachi:

"How shall we return?" (Mal. 3:7c) RSV

or in the words of the King James Version,

"Wherein shall we return" (Mal. 3:7c) RSV

In other words, they were asking in what manner had they sinned. What were they doing from which they should turn in order to be able to return to God? This strong note of Malachi resounded the prophetic message of old: the necessity of repentance and renewal because there would be judgment between the righteous and the wicked. Malachi realized that the religious life of the people was weak. He knew that since their spiritual vision was dim, the root of the existence of the nation was shaky. The weakened religious life directly affected both moral and social conditions. It was essential that the people return to God.

Malachi recognized the impudence of their spiritual pride. Their response to God's invitation revealed how their self-righteousness had blinded them. Either through blindness or through pretense they claimed no knowledge of shortcomings that called for repentance. Of all the detrimental forms of egotistical pride surely the worst is spiritual pride! A person who relaxes in the sunshine of his own self-approval, who recites his charities and pieties, who dwells on his excellent record versus that of his evil neighbors—this is the person who claims to be tolerant, generous, unbound by rules, and who thanks God for not being like others.

It is always easier for us to detect irregularities of the flesh than it is of the mind or spirit. It is less difficult to spot and condemn the boisterous alcoholic than it is to detect the person who is active and forthright in religious meetings but is underhanded, proud, and dishonest in his business during the week. We can more quickly recognize the person who has openly abandoned all sexual morality than we can the pious religious person who condemns the wickedness of the younger generation while he is desiring, if not actually involved in, secret adulterous relationships. We can recognize the person whose car or house denotes his vanity far quicker than we can detect the reason a person may seek places of leadership in his religious group to satisfy his pride, his hunger for acceptance, or his desire for recognition. We are quick to indict the person who accumulates and hoards his possessions and wealth, while we are not so insightful about greed that often possesses people active in religious circles, or even a church itself!

The third chapter of Genesis diagnosed pride as the parent sin. Man too often responds to the tendency to take what he wants, what he can, and make himself his own god. In this sense Adam is Everyman, and the experience of Adam is the universal experience of mankind. Adam willed himself to be removed from his subordinate relationship to God. It is this fundamental egotistical feeling in man that urges each of us to want to be first, to be independent of God and others, and to be self-sufficient.

It is frightening to consider that we modern Christians may be functioning more from the motives of Adam than out of submission to the Lordship of Jesus Christ. False spiritual pride may pump up our balloons of self-righteousness as we look around at others, thinking how much better we are than our neighbors. When a strong Word of God is uttered, we may tend to be glad that "those haughty sinners" had their toes stepped on without considering what God was saying to us. Self-seeking pride may cause us to be so boastful about attending worship on Sunday that we overlook or neglect how we live during the week in the world. Our presence in the place of worship may cause us to be condemnatory of those who are not like us, instead of our having such a significant encounter with God that we seek to extend his love to all he has created—without concern over whether they look, talk, act, or think as we do. Our pride over some minor accomplishment may blind us to the still-glaring weaknesses and needs in our lives.

For fear of causing a misunderstanding, it should be emphasized that a person of pride should not avoid entering a sanctuary. When all of us who have pride enter the house of God, there is the possibility we may experience such a revelation of God and such a realization of ourselves that renewal can take place in our lives. However, all religious persons should be cautioned to avoid the thought that simply in their going to a religious meeting all their spiritual needs are resolved. It simply does not happen automatically. There is a strong need for the fellowship of other believers and the inspiration of corporate worship. But if we fail to seek an encounter with God in the sanctuary, and if we fail to seek a transformed way of life in the world, then our attitude is not allowing us to be open to God's renewal in either the sanctuary or the world.

When we begin to recognize false pride in our lives, what can we do to rid ourselves of it? What is the source of renewal? How can we return to God? At the outset of seeking an answer we must realize there is no simple, easy, speedy remedy. Once a Puritan cried that getting rid of pride was like trying to peel an onion. Every time a skin was taken off, there still was another under it. It takes courage and sincerity to rip off the ugly facts about ourselves and unmask the pride engrained in us. But how can we get rid of pride? How can we as people who have not been fully committed to Christ, people who have not been possessed by God's purpose for us in the world, people who have often been more concerned about comfort and convenience than commitment and sacrifice—how can we be renewed in God?

Some of the popular ways churches are answering this compound question include the bus phenomenon. While this is a legitimate ministry in some instances, others are saying that by having a fleet of buses and a circus tent full of gimmicks to bring people in from everywhere, the church can be renewed. Others say renewal comes by moving out of an old location and establishing a church on new, more spacious, property. Still others advocate having a contest to secure a new publicity slogan for the church, one that will attract new members and bring new life. Some of us feel when all of the organizational wheels of the denomination are oiled and running smoothly, renewal will come. In recent years the advocates of small groups have asserted that their method is the only way for renewal to be experienced.

Are these really valid solutions for the need for renewal? They do not appear to be to me. There can be some good in any of the examples given, but not one of them is adequate when it alone or all of them together are offered as the source of renewal. In the last decade there has been a great deal of interest in and writing about both personal renewal and church renewal. But all the talking, all the writing, and all the grouping will not amount to a thing *unless the people involved repent and return to God!* Are many of us going through motions weekly that hinder renewal instead of aiding it? The story is told of a Sunday school teacher who, after telling the story about the proud Pharisee and the penitent publican, urged her class to thank God they were not like the Pharisee. Is this all our efforts at renewal achieve: an increase in our self-centered religious pride?

Is there an answer? Is there any source of renewal? Yes, there is, but it is not easy, quick, or cheap. Genuine renewal cannot be purchased on demand. We cannot earn it by obedience to a religious body or its leadership, regardless of how judgmental and dictatorial or how indifferent and nondemanding that leadership may be. The beginning of renewal is to see ourselves against some luminous background, to confront ourselves with the standard of excellence that puts our self-centeredness to shame.

This is what happens when we stand before the white, scorching purity of God in Jesus Christ. Then we can be open to repenting of our self-centered rebellions against God, our attempts to live apart from God. Then we can ask God to renew us with a right spirit, a right attitude, and a proper mode of living. There is no shortcut. Until we repent and return to God, until we ask for God's forgiveness and restoration to his intention for us in our creation, we will not experience reawakening or renewal.

We could walk down the aisle of a church weekly and there would be no difference in our lives unless we were willing to confess we had turned away from God, unless we sought his strength to return to him. Unquestionably this is a hard thing to do when our sin is not robbing a bank, depriving our family of food and shelter, embezzling from our company, living off nonmedical drugs, or participating in a group marriage. In our society today we need to realize that any form of self-centeredness is sin, any act of pride that separates us from God is wrong. Then we will be as willing and ready for renewal as the obvious social sinner.

Religious pride has eroded much of the power of God's Word. One has capsuled the need for renewal and the elimination of crippling pride in writing:

> Nothing would do more to rehabilitate Christianity in the general mind of the community and to command its respect than to have the rank and file of church people exhibit the cardinal virtues that underlie all true living, and make these the starting point for a further advance into the higher reaches of the religious experience.[3]

When we become aware of the tricks pride plays, we can open ourselves to God's strength and be ready to begin a growth experience in God.

Questions for Thought and Discussion

1. What is the difference between unhealthy pride and healthy self-esteem?
2. Why was repentance needed in the days of Malachi?
3. Why is repentance needed in our society today?
4. Does God change his attitude toward man? Explain.
5. In your moral system how do you compare sins of the flesh and sins of the mind or spirit?
6. In this chapter the view was expressed that because of weakened religious life, moral and social conditions are affected and a nation's very existence is shaken. Do you agree? Why or why not?

Suggestions for Action

1. When was the last time you looked at the sin in your life and repented before God? At the close of each day for a week, carefully try to enumerate the sins of action and thought, flesh, and mind and genuinely repent and ask for God's forgiveness and power to avoid these sins tomorrow. At the conclusion of the week evaluate your life to see if there has been any change in attitude and action as a result of your repentance.
2. Read either Robert J. McCracken's *What Is Sin? What Is Virtue?* (New York: Harper & Row, 1960) or Karl Menninger's *Whatever Became of Sin?* (New York: Hawthorn Books, 1973).
3. On page 81 several popular ways were listed by which modern churches are seeking renewal. By what means is your church seeking to enable individuals and the church to experience renewal? If a healthy approach to renewal is not being used, perhaps you might request either a group of leaders or a special study committee be given the task of working on this vital concern.

"Will man rob God? Yet you are robbing me. But you say, 'How are we robbing thee?' In your tithes and offerings. You are cursed with a curse, for you are robbing me; the whole nation of you. Bring the full tithes into the storehouse, that there may be food in my house; and thereby put me to the test, says the Lord of hosts, if I will not open the windows of heaven for you and pour down for you an overflowing blessing. I will rebuke the devourer for you, so that it will not destroy the fruits of your soil; and your vine in the field shall not fail to bear, says the Lord of hosts. Then all nations will call you blessed, for you will be a land of delight, says the Lord of hosts." (Mal. 3:8–12) RSV

8

The Most Unbelievable Theft

During the great wars of this century clothes have been col-
lected to aid the men in the armed forces. Time and again it
has been observed that coats would come in with all of the
buttons cut off. Supposedly generous people would decide
the buttons were good enough to be reused, so they would
snip them off and save them. In the process the gift of the
coat was made useless. Neither buttons nor the time was
available to repair the damage done to the coat. It is
unbelievable what some people will do in the name of giving
to someone else!

The famous violinist Fritz Kreisler died a few days before
his eighty-seventh birthday. At the age of seven he had been
the youngest child ever admitted to the Vienna Conservatory
of Music. In addition to his musical ability he spoke eight
languages and had a profound command of philosophy,
history, and mathematics. He was an outstanding violinist.
But even more significant, he was a remarkable man. He said
that he was born with music in him, a gift given by God. Just
as he did not acquire music, neither did he look on the money
he earned as his own. He called it "public money," a resource
entrusted to his care for proper distribution. He and his wife
sought to limit their needs to the bare minimum. They felt
morally guilty to go to a restaurant and order a costly meal,
for they realized in so doing they might deprive someone of a
piece of bread or a child of a bottle of milk. In spite of his

success he never built a home. He profoundly and humbly stated that between him and a home of his own stood all of the homeless in the world.[1]

Seemingly few people have assumed such an outlook on their lives and their possessions as did Fritz Kreisler. Statistics say that an increasing number of Americans commit theft each year, and many of them go free. And many thefts are never even reported. Of all the intricate thefts you have heard about, read about, or witnessed on the screen, which would you say was the greatest? It appears the greatest robbery of all is what we have done to God. Many of us have robbed God of our lives, just as countless persons did in the centuries before us. We have "cut off the buttons" of our gifts and shoved to God merely the worthless leftovers of our lives. We have grown so accustomed to ignoring God's claims on our lives that we would be shocked to think Malachi's words could apply to us when he says the people have robbed God (Mal. 3:8–12). No one seems to be shocked when we realize that we have withheld our tithes from him, and we do not expect anyone—the church treasurer, the finance committee, the board of deacons, the minister, even God himself—to do anything about it.

The story is told of a ten-year-old girl who went to church for the first time. When she came home, one of her neighbors asked her if she were good. She said not only was she good but she was also polite. She explained by saying when they passed the plate around with money in it, she did not take any. This seems to be the measuring stick by which most people determine whether or not they have robbed God. If they take nothing from the plate; if they receive nothing from observing corporate worship; if they participate in none of the learning, educating, or ministering functions of the church—they decide they owe God nothing and they have not robbed him of anything.

Before I did an in-depth study of Malachi, this passage was the only one I had ever heard taught or preached. In my mind Malachi was the book that said the tithe was to be brought to the church. But Malachi in its wholeness is a rich resource for revealing the Living Word of God for his people today. God desires the total stewardship of our lives entrusted to him. If a Christian's life is in proper order, then money will be in the right perspective. Stewardship, simply put, is a response to the good news of God's salvation. The giving of the tithe to God through the church continues to be an important part of our total stewardship.

A generation or two ago the church began to back away from teaching tithing, just as the church has often grown reluctant to teach the importance of precise, upright Christian morals for daily living. Many of today's churches are hesitant to speak out against anything that might keep them from getting new members or retaining their old ones. We get worked up about nonmedical drugs our youth use, but we are silent about the deadly menace of the most common drug, alcohol—we let AA say that! We call for bodily cleanliness and strength, but we are silent about the potential damage of tobacco—we let the surgeon general say that! We urge sexual purity and a high standard of morality, but we say nothing about dress styles, dating habits, or X-rated movies—we let the schools rule on them! We claim we want the needs of the whole man met so he will know the life God created him to live, but we are hesitant to get involved with ministering to people who do not act, think, look, and talk like we do—we let the government or community handle them!

With the people of Malachi's day we hear the question:

"Will man rob God?" (Mal. 3:8a) RSV

And we flinch with astonishment that a person would even consider such an evil deed! It is inconceivable, especially to "Christian people," that we would actually commit such a defraud of God. And we echo,

"How are we robbing thee?" (Mal. 3:8c) RSV

Malachi answered that we are robbing God by the tithes and offerings we have withheld. We have failed to bring the full, whole tithe to God. The giving of the tithe was part of the covenant relationship between God and the Hebrew people (Deut. 14:22ff; Lev. 27:30ff; Num. 18:21ff). Malachi indicted their failure to live up to the covenant. Jesus came saying he was not destroying but fulfilling the law and the prophets (Matt. 5:17). And he said that the righteousness of one who wished to enter the Kingdom of God should exceed that of the scribes and the Pharisees (Matt. 5:20). Tithing is part of the expectation, the responsibility, and the stewardship of a Christian.

The people accused of not giving their tithes were probably the skeptics who had blamed God for doing nothing and then had cut off their tithes. The world was not being run the way they wanted, the Temple was not functioning under their leadership, and the community was not answering to their whims—so they kept their money! This passage reenforces the people's need of repentance and return to God. Malachi urged the people to give their tithes both as a means and as an indication of their complete return. If they had not given their tithe due to disbelief in God, return to belief in him would have no finer symbol than the gift of their tithes.

Malachi's rationale for tithing seems to establish the basis for the tithe today. What is given is not as important as the attitude and priority in which it is given. God is concerned about the amount of the gift in relation to our means, but far more, he is concerned about us, the givers. People who are totally committed to God, to being a disciple of Christ, are also committed stewards of all they are and have. The tithe is neither the climax nor the sum total of stewardship. It is the beginning of stewardship, and it is an accurate indicator of the degree of the rest of our commitment as Christian stewards. If we pray for God's will to be done in our lives, we are asking for our hands as well as our pocketbooks to be opened.

We are among a generation of religious people who are more accustomed to praying than they are to giving. Our brand of Christianity is only partial allegiance instead of total life commitment.

> When you're asked to tithe and make a pledge
>   and you have to stop and ask what comes first
>   and you think of appliances you need
>   and you stop to consider the tax benefit
>   and you say a tenth is too legalistic
> So calculated giving becomes your method . . .
>   Your religion is going stale.[2]

The Persian king Xerxes, who led a great military expedition against the Greeks, once said: "Would that I had as many soldiers as I have men." Today's minister or religious leader might well exclaim: "Would that our church had as many givers as it has talkers!" Most Christians do not like to hear anything said about stewardship, particularly tithing, because they prefer to be urged toward devotionalism instead. There is nearly five times as much in the New Testament about stewardship as there is about prayer· The Christian faith is well capsuled in the verb *to give*. The Bible does not say that God loved the world so much that he promised, loaned, borrowed, withheld, hid, misused. . . . No, it tells us that he loved the world so much that he *gave* his Son to redeem us, to draw us unto himself in the Abundant Life (John 3:16). Jesus said we cannot serve both God and the world (Matt. 6:24). The worship of the world and its possessions always separates us from God. Our conversion to God must always include our possessions and our pocketbook!

Malachi declared that God challenged and invited us to be his partners in all the joys and privileges of his creation. He gave us health, vigor, vision, strength, and opportunity—all the basic needs of life. In essence God was saying that he blesses us in order that we might be a blessing to others. We are never to latch on to the foolish notion that we are the sole owner of what is in our possession. The deed is always held in God's hand. We are entrusted with the management of a part of God's creation. In the end we will be subjected to an accurate audit of how we have used what God gave us.

Like the people in Malachi's day, we are indicted by the loose manner in which many of us modern Christians deal with our plain obligations to the church we have pledged to support. The tithe and total stewardship were part of the covenantal agreement between God and the Hebrew people. The church has looked at the tithe as part of its agreement between its members and God, but we have ignored this fact, forgotten it, or hidden it for fear that such a pronouncement might scare off a prospective member or create even more inactive ones. One student of the prophet described almost every contemporary church member when he wrote that "the work and support of a church is borne by one-third of its congregation; another third looks on; and the remaining third does not know what it is all about."[3] Can we not understand how we are robbing God? Church members not only rob God of the tithe, but they also rob him through lack of personal commitment and loyalty, haphazard church attendance, indifference toward public worship, and failure to identify with and participate in the church's mission in God's world. It is with this view of the church a poet penned the words:

> Like a Freshman forum
> Moves the Church of God;
> Brothers we are talking
> Where the saints have trod.
> We are not decided
> Whether we shall be

We often hear the youth of our society belittled. Yet I have had students talk with me about their desire to minister to others and to raise money to help others. Recently students have asked for help to minister to prisoners, provide food for the hungry, and aid the underprivileged. Many of our youth are interested in helping others, but their task is difficult because of lack of funds. We, the church, are letting the government or community do what the church should be doing, because we dare to rob God of our money, energy, leadership, and ideas. We give more of ourselves to earning a living than we do to acknowledging Christ as our Lord. We give more of ourselves and our money to our favorite civic club or community concern than we do to Christ and his church. We spend more time and money in our social club than we do for our Lord. We contribute more financial support and enthusiasm and incur more expenses with our favorite ball team than we give to support the proclamation of Christ and the ministry of his church.

Yet we dare ask how we have robbed God? We rob God when we fail to give him a tithe, which is a symbol of the gift of our whole life. All the rest of our possessions should be used wisely under his guidance, including the natural resources we use, the environment we enjoy, and the property and money we have. All of our abilities, influence, and time should be invested in his purpose for our lives. Our blessing in tithing is that our spiritual lives—our relation to God and our realization of our purpose in creation—will be enriched when we joyfully acknowledge our indebtedness to God for all of life. This is what we do when we return directly to God that which he has asked of us.

If we now understand clearly how we rob God, we must answer why we fail to be committed stewards, why we fail to give the tithe, the symbol of our lives, as well as our very lives themselves. Many of us grew up with the feeling of always being in debt. That experience has left different kinds of marks on the people who lived in difficult days. There were things my family wanted to buy that we had to wait for—wait until some things were paid off or wait until more money was available. Frequently the "until" never seemed to come. The emergencies, the unexpected things, kept me, a minister's child, fearful of indebtedness. I grew up among coal miners who never escaped debt. Between paydays they received company credit for necessities at high prices and high interest. When they were paid, there was never enough to cover the company's charges. Most of them had integrity with their indebtedness, as Tennessee Ernie Ford described years ago in his ballad "Sixteen Tons."

The integrity of my father in the Kentucky coalfields following the economic recession of the late 1940s still stands out in my mind. Many of his friends filed bankruptcy, but my father eventually repaid all his creditors. Throughout my years at home his tithe was joyfully given—not begrudgingly, not to earn God's favor, not to get our family material things—but because he found joy in acknowledging his indebtedness to God, from whom all his blessings came. The Old Testament people emphasized the material blessings for the tithe because they had no concept of life beyond this. It was Christ who affirmed the endless life of the Christian disciple. Christ assured us that the future is in God's hands. When I attempt to write about tithing, I do not say it gives material blessings. I interpret the mind-set of Malachi in light of two factors. One is the New Testament's proclamation that there is more to be than this life; the other is my own father, who joyfully tithed but still knew financial problems. We need not worry if the wicked seem to prosper now. Eventually we all will have to give answer to God for the kind of stewards we have been with our total lives.

My father helped me learn integrity with money, and he enabled me to know joy in giving to God. And this is far more important than giving me things he could not for lack of money—things such as new cars, expensive clothes, nice trips, elaborate parties, a free ticket through college and graduate school. And I would not trade my gifts of integrity and joy for anything!

Most all of us fear debt. So we say we cannot afford to tithe. We claim we want to be able to pay all of our bills. Actually we are saying we do not want to be indebted to God. We are implying we want to live life on our own. But life simply is not that way! We are the creation of God. We cannot be cut off from him and still know the fullness of life. Bishop Gerald Kennedy noted: "Christianity is a proclamation that we are always in debt and service to our brethren is our privilege."[5] Our tithes and offerings given to God are our privilege, as well as what is expected of us by God. Lest we forget, when we accepted God's call in Christ, we also accepted responsibility. We made an agreement with God in Christ that involves the commitment of all of our life. Tithing is our responsibility and is a means whereby the individual and the Christian community bear witness to the world. People apart from God see not only the joy of tithers but also the ministry done through our efforts.

Tithing is also a tangible means of expressing gratitude to God for all his matchless grace to us in Jesus Christ. It is an outgrowth of what has happened to the heart. When Christ has truly touched the heart, the pocketbook will most assuredly be dedicated to his work in the world. God's generosity in Jesus Christ motivates generosity in the authentic Christian. Christians who take their faith seriously need no coercion to give their money to God through Christ's church. One minister relates that a new member came to see him to ask about the church's needs. After outlining the annual budget the minister told the member what the average amount was that each member contributed. The man looked in astonishment as he told his minister that becoming a disciple of Christ and joining the church comprised one of the greatest decisions of his life. Because it meant so much he announced that his annual gift would be a sum that far exceeded the average contribution. The startled minister murmured that he was very generous only to hear the vibrant Christian reply, "God has been very generous to me."[6]

We can continue to participate in the most unbelievable theft of God. But we should hear a word of warning: "A secularized and worldly church may well see its spiritual heritage taken from it and vested in some alien society."[7] Centuries ago Goethe declared that "a nation can endure anything except continuous prosperity." Why? We have failed to learn the lesson that being a steward is a partnership with God. Material things tend to take over in prosperity, and God is left out. We need to grow in our total stewardship, and we need to give a tithe of our increase, not because God needs the money, not to do God a favor, but because

> we need to give
> we need to try to eliminate our selfishness,
> we need to abandon our attempts to be independent of God.

We are appalled at the unbelievable thefts of others. Now in light of Malachi's Word of God, we have to decide about our lives in relation to God. Hopefully we will hear God's Word directed to *us*. And may we be consistent in the standards we expect of others and in the standards we expect of ourselves!

Questions for Thought and Discussion

1. What was your attitude toward the people who cut off the buttons from coats they donated to the needy?

2. Do you recognize times when you have robbed from God? How did you feel then? How do you feel now?

3. Are you individually, and is your church collectively,

guilty of sidestepping important biblical teachings of life's stewardship for fear of offending persons or losing members?

4. Is God more concerned about the gift or the giver? Does each have a place? Explain your answer.

5. How did you feel when you read there is five times as much in the New Testament about stewardship as there is about prayer?

6. How do you view the total stewardship of your Christian life?

7. In light of your study of the text of Malachi and this chapter, how do you define the tithe?

8. Do you tithe?

Suggestions for Action

1. Make a two-week inventory of the use of your time. As nearly as possible, summarize on paper how you use each half hour of your time. At the end of the two weeks, analyze the stewardship of your life, including how much time was spent in acknowledging God's place in your life, in enriching your relationship with him, or in giving thanks for his gifts to you.

2. If you are contributing less than 10 percent of your income to your church, commit yourself for a month to give a tithe. At the conclusion of the month evaluate what you gave up in order to give the tithe. Determine which is more important for the future. Remind yourself that while God expects the tithe, he also anticipates a joyful, willing giver.

"Your words have been stout against me, says the Lord. Yet you say, 'How have we spoken against thee?' You have said 'It is vain to serve God. What is the good of our keeping his charge or of walking as in mourning before the Lord of hosts? Henceforth we deem the arrogant blessed; evildoers not only prosper but when they put God to the test they escape.'"

Then those who feared the Lord spoke with one another; the Lord heeded and heard them, and a book of remembrance was written before him of those who feared the Lord and thought on his name. "They shall be mine, says the Lord of hosts, my special possession on the day when I act, and I will spare them as a man spares his son who serves him. Then once more you shall distinguish between the righteous and the wicked, between one who serves God and one who does not serve him."
(Mal. 3:13–18) RSV

9

Whose Are You?

It is told that Dr. Albert Schweitzer would often ask a person passing by to assist him with a broken or bleeding person in Africa. The response was usually negative, for the person would declare that the distressed victim was not a member of his tribe. This reaction raises a very penetrating question: What is the real worth of others? Are some in the human family worth more in the sight of God than others?

The ready feedback of most Christians is that God so loved the whole world. . . . It is on the basis of his great love that he calls us who are blessed by him to become a blessing to others, to extend his love to all men everywhere. How can we accomplish this aim? Do we love merely by saying words? No! We love

> by giving ourselves—
> by teaching,
> touching,
> sharing,
> caring,
> giving,
> living,
> speaking,
> listening,
> crying,
> laughing—
> by letting Christ live out his ministry through us.

This kind of love is not easy to appropriate in our lives! When Paul wrote of godlike love, (*agape*) (1 Cor. 13), he was not referring to some sweet-smelling, luxurious, slick robe of self-righteous piety. This love is the consistently working, back-aching, brow-sweating daily fare of the person who loves others as Christ loves us.

The improper witness of those Africans with whom Albert Schweitzer worked leads us to the setting of the eighth rhetorical question Malachi raised in God's behalf. Previously seven improper aspects of the religious life of the prophet's contemporaries—and people today—were pinpointed. They were

> improper attitude,
> improper prayer,
> improper sacrifice and commitment,
> improper family relations,
> improper discernment,
> improper sense of security, and
> improper stewardship.

The final part of the book of Malachi gives his indictment for people who have an improper witness. He speaks for the Lord, saying:

> "*Your words have been stout against me.* . . . *Yet you say, 'How have we spoken against thee?'* You have said, 'It is vain to serve God. What is the good of our keeping his charge or of walking as in mourning before the Lord of hosts? Henceforth we deem the arrogant blessed; evildoers not only prosper, but when they put God to the test, they escape.' " (Mal. 3:13–15)

The people were "being hard on God" with the language they used, with the accusations they made, and with their questioning of the very character of God. Since Malachi had already denounced the hard cynics (Mal. 2:17–3:5), it seems that these doubters, these false witnesses, had once been the godly of the land who, because of the existing conditions, become doubtful. They were questioning the whole wisdom of practicing religion and blaming God for being indifferent toward their religious acts. It was in this mood that the people were ignoring God's commandments and failing to be penitent for their sins. After all, the arrogant evildoers were prospering! The people had done everything it appeared they should have done. They should have been entitled to God's blessings, for the righteous were supposed to be rewarded with prosperity and the faithless were to be punished with adversity (Deut. 28). But this was not the case now. The people had come to believe there were no benefits to be gained by serving God. Surely dealing with the problem of the prosperity and well-being of the wicked is common to religious people of every age.

What is the outcome of such an attitude among those supposed people of God? They were having an adverse witness both to those within their nation and to those beyond them. There they were, the religious people, saying stout, hard, strong, harsh things against God! How could the love and concern of God come through the instrument of people who were harsh skeptics? They belittled the name of God, took God's name in vain, and did not hold up God to be the true, righteous God. They were called and blessed by God so that they might be a blessing to others. Basically they failed God then and have tended to fail him over the centuries.

What about Christians standing in the tradition of the people of God who worshipped him before Christ? Whose are you? What kind of witness to God are you giving today? What does being a Christian mean to your day-by-day living? Who knows you are a Christian? William Stringfellow, a Christian lawyer in New York City's East Harlem, writes that he knew a New York clergyman who was pressured into leaving his work because his superiors criticized him for being too specialized and for taking too much of his time away from his church members. The minister was informed that

> he spent too much time with people, especially with some who were junkies or prostitutes or colored or poor or otherwise "undesirable." What happened to him is a measure of how deeply estranged the churches are from the world—and from Christ. What happened to him is a sign of how embarrassing the Gospel has become to the churches.[1]

If we who are Christians are going to give a genuine, authentic witness of God in Christ, we are going to have to live in the world where Christ lives! We are going to have to take our rightful places in the world with Christ in us!

During the Middle Ages the Christian people largely retreated from the world and lived apart from it. Monks were a very popular breed in those centuries that span a thousand years. Since the Reformation, over four centuries ago, the word has been proclaimed that Christians should be actively involved in the world as Christ's followers. It frequently seems that communication is slow to get around to everyone! Many Christians in the last quarter of the twentieth century are still trying to isolate their "religious lives" from the rest of life. They are trying to divide their "happy, worldly lives" from their "serious, religious lives." Most Christians today are confronted by religious groups that are largely separated from the world, afraid of the world, unprepared for and uninterested in witnessing to and ministering in the world. This is true because for too long these ecclesiastical groups have been comprised of members who wanted to escape the world. As Stringfellow analyzed:

> These churches more and more retreat into themselves. They become so inverted, so caught up in internal

maintenance and procedure, so entrapped in preserving and proliferating a cumbersome, costly, self-serving, officious, indulgent, soft ecclesiastical apparatus that it becomes easy to think that they don't have to care about the world any more since they are so much consumed in caring for themselves.[2]

We give a distorted, improper witness of God's Word when we imply that any religious group can be separated from the world and that the individual Christian or a church has a reason for existing apart from caring for the world in Christ's name. Once a woman commented to her minister that she thought their church would have to start having bingo parties because their attendance had dropped off so much. That minister retorted by saying he hoped God would forbid they should ever resort to any trickery, manipulation, force, or commercialism to con people into the experience of church—its

> mission,
> ministry,
> worship,
> education, or
> high calling in Christ Jesus our Lord.

We are not asked to flash a membership card from an exclusive club. We are asked to bear a cross in the name of Christ!

The week after preaching a message on witnessing, a minister received a letter from a worshiper. She accused him of making it too easy for the worshipers, offering God's forgiveness for their lack of action. She concluded by writing: "Please don't let us leave church comfortable. We need encouragement to go out and love people in the ways that are not easy."[3] Bold, courageous witnesses are needed in the world, and the church can encourage its members to be this kind of Christian disciple.

It was interesting to note the stages of the challenging book *In But Not Of the World*, written by the late Robert Spike. When it was reprinted, it came out under the title *Tests of a Living Church*. If we reflect on the two titles, we can see they fit nicely together. The tests of a living church are centralized in the issue of whether or not it is in but not of the world. In spite of our weaknesses the church is still important and necessary as an instrument of the proclamation of God's love and mercy. If we are genuine Christians and become committed church members who can honestly confess our weaknesses, perhaps we can become freer to be involved in the delicate and time-consuming work of genuine evangelism. If we think we live in a nation that is basically Christian with isolated spots of secularism, then we can throw out snappy talk about the benefits of our church and be quite in order. But if we recognize that ours is not really a Christian nation, that there are floating in an immense sea of humanity only isolated islands of Christian culture, we might affirm the lifelong task of giving witness to Christ to the people in the world beyond our own religious community.

This kind of evangelism takes into account that genuine communication between people in our day is becoming very difficult and often desperately unsuccessful. Only the Christian persons who are willing to be completely authentic, open, and honest in the world can be evangelists today. We cannot talk about the meaning and power of Christ unless he is effective in our daily living. We must be willing to acknowledge our weakness, our sin, when we are telling others that Christ seeks to forgive human sin.

Tennessee Williams highlights Big Daddy in his drama *Cat on a Hot Tin Roof*. Big Daddy was the father who was successful in the world because he never confused the truth with tradition or public manners. His son, Brick, was a young man who was an alcoholic wreck before the age of thirty because he had not been able to accept the distinction between truth and public manners. Big Daddy, afraid he had terminal cancer, told his son that "the human animal is a beast that dies and if he's got money he buys and buys and buys and I think the reason he buys everything he can buy is that in the back of his mind he has the crazy hope that one of his purchases will be life everlasting!—which it can never be."[4]

More often than we realize or are willing to admit, people outside the established religious communities are honestly seeking an encounter with a God who will transform their lives. Our witness means nothing if no one knows we are Christians or if the supposed Christian witness we offer is feebly improper—a hindrance rather than a help to the cause of Christ. Christianity, in its truest sense, is witness. Christian discipleship involves one beggar telling another where to get food. The Christian does not look down on others and offer them something out of his bounty. He has no bounty! A Christian witness stands alongside one who does not know God's love and points to the whole action of God in Christ Jesus.

You may be asking yourself why should you bother with talking about Christian witnessing when your faith, like that of Malachi's contemporaries, has gone stale. One writer captured the emotions of many people in the twentieth century when he wrote:

> When Monday arrives and the world rushes in
> and Paul is displaced by a news headline
> and yesterday's sermon was about . . . ?
> and making a living becomes your concern
> So you forget about how to live . . .
> Your religion is going stale.[5]

One other verse of Malachi speaks prominently to us:

Then those who feared the Lord spoke with one another. . . . (Mal. 3:16) RSV

It appears that either this group maintained their faith in God, or through their doubting and questioning they developed a more mature faith in God. Very likely it was during this time of great doubt these believers came together, joined forces, sought to strengthen one another's faith, and attempted to counteract the rapid spread of skepticism. Rather than accusing God, they waited patiently for God's manifestation in his own time. Malachi affirmed that God will remember those who are truly righteous and will bring healing and salvation.

We, the people of God, can click our heels with joy when we realize the future is in God's hands! Both the righteous and the wicked will have to stand before God. There is no need for us to become overwrought by who gets what now. Our energy and concern should be directed toward the spread of the love of God in his world.

Our witness to others is never effective for long if all we offer them is the religion we have inherited. People neither want nor need hand-me-downs. They do need a vital, personal experience with God in Christ. A witness who merely invites those who are not Christians to come join his religious group is not a strong witness. A person who thinks that his religious life will be set right simply by joining a church will soon be in for a rude awakening that may cause him to reject God altogether. A witness who lives out the love of Christ in his life and then invites and encourages one to know and experience God in the midst of a Christian community of faith—this is a genuine, authentic witness who is an instrument of pointing others to God in Christ, not to man.

We must be careful that we modern Christians are not

directing all our energy toward getting people into our buildings and our membership. We must develop an awareness of our responsibility to identify with the life that is being lived all around us. Then we need to offer intercessory prayer for those who do not know Christ, for all the Christian witnesses, and for patience to be led by his Spirit. This kind of prayer leads us away from being defensive and withdrawn from the world and helps us become vital witnesses in the world. On this basis we can demonstrate that we want the world to know whose we are—that we belong to Christ and that we are not ashamed to bear his name. We give witness to Christ's Lordship not only in foreign lands but also in every corner of our nation—in our home, in our neighborhood, and in our county and city.

In spite of our greater understanding of human makeup we often do not seek to understand the total person and speak to that person. While there are a few who are too pious and religiously talkative, most of us have camped on the other extreme.

> Our reticence becomes studied silence. We become too self-conscious, too shy to speak freely about religion, particularly to those closest to us. It is hard to learn to speak simply, naturally, directly, and without affectation about religion to those whom one knows best; but we should discipline ourselves in this delicate art.[6]

One way we can strengthen our witness is by sharing with and gaining strength from other Christians. In the difficult days for our nation and world we who love the Lord need to speak often with one another. The authentic witnesses of God were strengthened in this manner in Malachi's day, and the same can be true for us today.

The prophet Malachi has raised God's questions and answers in such an effective manner that they still speak directly and forcefully to God's people today. As you read and reread the words of the prophet, may you be challenged and renewed by his insights. On the basis of God's Living Word, may you gain greater strength from God and from the Christian community for living out your life more effectively in God's world. Only then will people know whose you are and discover your God for their own personal God.

Questions for Thought and Discussion

1. Do your contemporaries blame God for their troubles, i.e., sickness, death of loved ones, financial problems, family strife, etc.? If yes, why?

2. In the Old Testament there was the concept that the righteous were rewarded with prosperity and the wicked with adversity. Did this view hold true throughout the Old Testament? Do people today believe this? Do you? Why or why not?

3. Realizing that many religious people separate their "religious lives" from their "worldly lives," how do you view your life in its totality? Evaluate whether or not a person can be "Christian" just in church buildings and religious meetings.

4. What methods are used by your church to draw people to participate in the Christian learning, worshiping, ministering, and witnessing?

5. What kind of witness of God in Christ does your life give?

6. How do you show whose you are?

Suggestions for Action

1. If your church does not have a missions committee, work with your minister and church leaders in an effort to

establish one. The purpose of this group would include coordinating the mission projects of the church, making members aware of needs, enlisting support for local mission projects, training people for specific mission tasks, leading the church to reach out its ministry into the community, and reminding the entire church that its basic purpose is to be on mission. If your church has such a committee, find a specific way in which you can work with it and support it.

2. During the next three months, seek out a person who does not know Christ as Lord. If you are not aware of someone, ask your minister or education leader for the name of a non-Christian. Begin or strengthen a friendship with that person. On the basis of your genuine concern and trust, share verbally what the Lordship of Christ means to your joy and fulfillment in living. Do not become dismayed if the person does not agree with you. Try to keep a positive witness by your words and your life before the person. Let God's Spirit work through your love, concern, and witness. Hopefully the person will accept Christ as Lord. But regardless of the response, you will have been faithful to Christ's call by declaring boldly and directly whose you are.

3. If your church does not have any regular training offered for witnessing, request that such opportunities be offered to all the members. Staff members or lay persons may be qualified to lead it, or outside resource persons might be brought in to facilitate the training. Attempt to see that not only are your fellow members made aware of the need for a vital witness, but also that insights, encouragement, and direction are provided for that witness. Frequently a lay witness given in worship followed by an informal talk-back can be most helpful and stimulating to the church at large.

4. If you have done this study in a group, evaluate its effectiveness in providing you strength from other Christians. If you have not had a group experience, ask your church leadership to establish the means whereby you and your fellow Christians can participate in various short-term study-sharing groups.

Notes

FOREWORD

"Malachi," Earl Marlatt, *Cathedral* (New York: Harper & Brothers, 1937), copyright by Earl Marlatt.

PREFACE

1. The eight focal passages of Malachi in his question-and-answer style are 1:2, 1:6, 1:7 and 1:13a, 2:14, 2:17, 3:7, 3:8, and 3:13. I am indebted to Dr. John Joseph Owens, Professor of Old Testament at Southern Baptist Seminary, Louisville, Kentucky, who lectured on this concept of Malachi in a 1972 Continuing Theological Education conference.

CHAPTER 1

1. George Adam Smith, *The Book of the Twelve Prophets*, vol. 2 (New York: Doubleday, Doran, 1929), pp. 334–35.
2. Phillips Brooks, *Christ the Life and Light*, selected from writings of Phillips Brooks by W.M.L. Jay (New York: E.P. Dutton, 1905), pp. 174ff.
3. J.B. Phillips, *Your God Is Too Small* (New York: Macmillan, 1963), p.v.

CHAPTER 2

1. John Steinbeck, *To a God Unknown* (New York: Viking Press, 1958), pp. 180–181.
2. Helmut Thielicke, *I Believe: The Christian's Creed*, trans. John W. Doberstein and H. George Anderson (Philadelphia: Fortress Press, 1968), p. x.
3. Frederick Carl Eiselen, *Commentary on the Old Testament*, vol. IX (New York: Eaton & Mains, 1907), p. 709.
4. A. Leonard Griffith, *Barriers to Christian Belief* (New York: Harper & Row, 1969), p. 39.
5. Archbishop François Fenelon cited in "We Need New Ways to Pray," Ardis Whitman, *Reader's Digest*, December 1969, p. 79.

CHAPTER 3

1. Robert Bolt, *A Man for All Seasons* (New York: Vintage Books, 1962), p. 81.
2. Tennessee Williams, *Cat on a Hot Tin Roof* (New York: New American Library, 1955), p. 79.

3. Ibid., p. 94

4. Willard L. Sperry, "Malachi," *The Interpreter's Bible*, vol. 6 (New York: Abingdon Press, 1956), p. 1127.

5. Samuel Taylor Coleridge, "The Ancient Mariner," pt. 3, lines 143–46.

6. T. Miles Bennett, "Malachi," *Broadman Bible Commentary*, vol. 7 (Nashville: Broadman Press, 1972), p. 383.

CHAPTER 4

1. Ernest Fremont Tittle, *The Foolishness of Preaching* (New York: Henry Holt, 1930), p. 301.

2. Steinbeck, p. 47.

3. Bennett, p. 377.

4. Stephen Neill, *On the Ministry* (London: SCM Press, 1952), p. 54.

5. Richard Baxter, *The Reformed Pastor* (London: Epworth Press, 1950), p. 158.

6. Robert W. Bailey, "The Revitalization of the Preaching Event with Emphasis on Lay Participation and Perception," (S.T.D. diss., Southern Baptist Theological Seminary, Louisville, Kentucky, 1970), pp. 47–50.

7. Kyle E. Haselden, *The Urgency of Preaching* (New York: Harper & Row, 1963), pp. 102–106.

8. John Henry Jowett, *The Preacher: His Life and Work* (New York: Harper & Brothers, 1912), p. 10.

9. Steinbeck, p. 49.

10. James T. Cleland, *Preaching to Be Understood* (New York: Abingdon Press, 1965), p. 110.

11. Wallace Fisher, *Preaching and Parish Renewal* (New York: Abingdon Press, 1966), pp. 24–25.

CHAPTER 5

1. Max Frisch, *Andorra*, from *Three Plays* (London: Methuen, 1962), pp. 182, 204, 225ff, 251ff.

2. Elton and Pauline Trueblood, *The Recovery of Family Life* (New York: Harper & Row, 1953), pp. 43–48.

3. Ibid., p. 19.

4. Gibson Winter, *Love and Conflict* (Garden City, N.Y.: Doubleday, 1961), p. 90.

5. Howard and Charlotte Clinebell, *The Intimate Marriage* (New York: Harper & Row, 1970), p. 9.

6. Arthur Miller, *Death of a Salesman* (New York: Viking Press, 1967), p. 138.

CHAPTER 6

1. Judea was under the rule of Alexander himself from 333 to 323 B.C., when Alexander died. One of his generals, Ptolemy Lagi, then took over and founded the Ptolemaic dynasty, which ruled until 198 B.C. Then the shift was made to another Greek dynasty, the Seleucids, who were descended from Seleucus, another of Alexander's generals.

NOTES

2. James A. Michener, *The Source* (New York: Random House, 1965), pp. 313ff.

3. Bennett, p. 387.

4. M. Thomas Starkes, "The World Tomorrow?" Home Mission Board, Southern Baptist Convention, Atlanta, Ga., February 2, 1972, pp. 1ff.

5. Harold P. Simonson, ed., *Selected Writings of Jonathan Edwards* (New York: Frederick Ungar, 1970), p. 102.

6. Robert C. Dentan, "Malachi," *The Interpreter's Bible*, vol. 6 (New York: Abingdon Press, 1956), p. 1138.

7. Raymond Calkins, *The Modern Message of the Minor Prophets* (New York: Harper & Brothers, 1947), p. 139.

8. Sperry, p. 1139.

CHAPTER 7

1. Robert J. McCracken, *What Is Sin? What Is Virtue?* (New York: Harper & Row, 1966), p. 14.

2. Bennett, p. 390.

3. Calkins, p. 139.

CHAPTER 8

1. James Hastings, ed., *The Great Texts of the Bible*, vol. 17 (Aberdeen, Scotland: The Speaker's Bible Office, 1930), p. 128.

2. William G. Hurt, "Malachi: When Religion Goes Stale," *The Religious Herald*, September 20, 1973, p. 14.

3. Calkins, p. 140.

4. Charles L. Wallis, *A Treasury of Sermon Illustrations* (New York: Abingdon Press, 1950), p. 70.

5. Gerald Kennedy, *Fresh Every Morning* (New York: Harper & Row, 1966), p. 20.

6. Leonard Griffith, *God's Time and Ours* (New York: Abingdon Press, 1964), p. 198.

7. Sperry, p. 1129.

CHAPTER 9

1. William Stringfellow, *A Private and Public Faith* (Grand Rapids, Mich.: Wm. B. Eerdmans, 1962), p. 75.

2. Ibid., p. 74.

3. Robert A. Raines, *The Secular Congregation* (New York: Harper & Row, 1968), p. 60.

4. Williams, p. 67.

5. Hurt, p. 14.

6. Sperry, p. 1142.